SHE'S PREGNANT AND YOU'RE SCREWED

Will Vernon
She's Pregnant and You're Screwed
One man's memoirs

Published by BooxAi
ISBN:978-965-578-856-3

SHE'S PREGNANT AND YOU'RE SCREWED

One man's memoirs

WILL VERNON

Contents

INTRODUCTION   vii

OH NO...!!!   1
YIN   4
HOW I CAME TO WRITE THIS BOOK   6
THE "FUN" HERD EFFECT   17
THE MENTAL MIRROR   18
BUYER'S REMORSE   20
THE ITCHING FEELING   21
WHEN IT HITS   23
AND THERE YOU HAVE IT   26
TRUTH BE TOLD   27
WHAT YOU NEEDED TO HEAR   28
CHAOS THEORY   30
INK TO PAPER   32
REMEMBERING   34
BECAUSE OTHERS HAVE SAID SO...   36
BETWEEN THE LINES   38
PERSONAL DEVELOPMENT   39
...HAPPY WITH OTHERS   41
EDUCATIONAL DEVELOPMENT   44
THE HUMAN FACTOR   48
FUEL YOUR MIND   52
INSPIRE AND BE INSPIRED   54
D.I.E   57
GOOD DIE YOUNG   60
"REACH FOR THE MOON, AND IF YOU
MISS AT LEAST YOU'LLBE UPON THE
STARS"...   62
LES BROWN
WHY IS IT?   64
AH-HA MOMENT   66
KEEPING IT SIMPLE   68
JUST START   71

YANG 73
JUST AROUND THE CORNER 74
WHAT A WASTE 76
A SHOE BOX WORTH MORE THAN A
MILLION DOLLARS 78
AN APPLE 80
WHO AM I? 82
COMMUNICATION AND SELF-
PROJECTION 85
THINK BIG, AND IF IT'S NOT OUT
THERE, THEN CREATE IT 86
APPLYING KNOWLEDGE; BEING THE
EXAMPLE!! 91
HEALTH AND EXERCISE 95
DIET 96
EXERCISE 98
HAVE FUN 100
WHEN YOU HAVE A MILLION-DOLLAR
VISION, DON'T SURROND YOURSELF
WITH ONE-CENT MINDS 102
CHILDREN'S COLLAGE 105
BILLS 106
SAVE 107
INVEST 109
DONATING 113
WHEN ARGUMENTS HAPPEN 116
PART NEGATIVE 118
LEAVE IT BEHIND 120
MILITARY VETERAN LESSON 122
GROWTH 124
CHANGING THOUGHT 127
TREE THEORY 129
CONFUSION VS DISCIPLINE 132
IT'S NEVER TOO LATE TO CHANGE 134
THE TRUE COST 136

INTRODUCTION

Inspiration looks different for everyone. I do not know what may inspire you, but I hope you start finding some inspiration throughout this book. I wrote this book about seven years ago, and kept playing with it, questioning whether if it's too short or good enough. As I watch the world around us change, it dawned on me that this book will act as a reference guide, a guide that inspires you to dig deeper into yourself.

It's human nature to not want to be alone. I share throughout this book my thoughts throughout my darkest moments, and the desire and spark that helped drive the philosophies that pulled me through with hope that you realize that you are not alone in your darkest moments.

As you will read, it all started with a trip to the mailbox and an extract on disk by Jim Rohn. It is important to know your roots, and for personal development, Jim Rohn was that for me. Many philosophers, thinkers, motivational speakers all have one or two books, seminars, or sayings that they hold on too, and I am no exception.

I have been blessed with two great children, and the influence and encouragement of great women who without them, I would still be pondering if publishing these thoughts would be worth it. If this book inspires one person, changes the life of one person, helps one person achieve their dreams or helps them out of a metaphorical hole, then it is absolutely worth it.

She's Pregnant and You're Screwed isn't a step-by-step self-help guide. It's a book about the feelings of fear, hopelessness, and panic, and how to attack it. It's a recognition of our deepest thoughts. It drives home the good and bad and serves as a thought-provoking manual of ideas that may inspire change within you.

As I look to embark on the next chapter of my life, I hope to reach thousands, even millions of people, to inspire change and spark a new light within their hearts and minds. I will leave you with this. During the summer of 2021 whilst I was living with a dear friend of mine, I had promised my daughter that we would do a bunch of things the following day. The next morning him and I were talking and my daughter walks out of her bedroom all excited and said, "it's tomorrow". My friend and I looked at one another as this inspired a new way of thinking. My daughter was right, it was tomorrow, and why wait any longer. It's a message that I've been pondering on how to inspire to people. I believe it starts with She's Pregnant and You're Screwed, yet I ask you to watch this space as ITS TOMORROW.

Will Vernon

OH NO...!!!

She's pregnant and you're screwed was the exact thought I had when I found out I was going to be a dad again. This wasn't the first time I had felt that icky, sickening feeling, and it surely won't be the last. No matter what I was doing, this feeling kept creeping up on me. She whispered in my thoughts and forced my hand, changing any direction I was going. Everywhere I looked she stood, staring at me. She would tell me everything I did was wrong. She hid whatever goals I hoped to achieve from me. Each time I swiped my bank card, her voice was clearer than crisp, informing me that I shouldn't purchase whatever item I was attempting to buy. As I drove by multiple gyms, she stood guard at their doors with no key in sight. All my energy and time had once again disappeared, and I was to never again regain control.

She has many names, many faces, and she sends many to an early grave. She's cruel, unfair, and knocks the strongest to their knees in the blink of an eye. Fear, doubt, and the impossible are just a few of her identities. Many people close their eyes hoping to avoid her. She exists with a persistent clarity that not only wants to take me down, but everyone that stands on her path.

I wondered for many years how many people felt her. Did other people see her like I did or was it just me suffering from this immense pain? Was I being punished for being too scared to man up and be a father to a beautiful daughter? Did she steal business ventures away from others or was it only me she sent the masses to mock my ideas?

She was the gun to my head when depression hit me. I gained weight and struggled to get through each day. Everyone else seemed to be okay. Everyone else seemed to have answers. I truly felt like I was the only person to see her. She's dark and cold and would keep me up at night. She placed beers in my hand promising me that answers lay deep at the bottom. She took my money, stole my son, and made sure that I was involved in arguments daily. The pain is unbearable as she drives a stake right through your heart.

It seemed to me that no one else stood on her path, and I didn't know how to get off. Occasionally, I would close my eyes, but my mind was corrupted by darkness. She wouldn't leave me alone, and there was no passing her off. Within the shadows of my thoughts drummed a beat of hope. A small distant beat that if I truly concentrated hard enough, a blurry vision of sound that shined through a disarray of space.

Just as easy as she could pierce your heart, a beat from the drum could pierce your mind. All you have to do is keep listening. I truly don't know why it happens this way and some days I truly don't care. Cruelty seeks a man to latch onto, and as I was soon to discover, I wasn't alone. Many people had seen her, and to my surprise, defeated her. Life works in mysterious ways, and behind every mystery lies a path. Every breathing soul on this Earth stands on her path which is life. As I was soon to discover, life could be grasped with a fist of might, will of God, and the single beat of a drum.

She was sure that I would never regain control and now my drum deafens her every sound. I stand tall knowing that if life takes a swipe at my knees, I'll be sure to jump. She may surely exist, but so do I. Inside this book lay the ideas, philosophies, and disciplines that changed my life. It is my wish to share them with you so when she comes lurking in the depths of your mind, you too can defeat her.

YIN

(I n Chinese philosophy) the passive female principle of the universe, characterized as female and sustaining and associated with earth, dark, and cold.

As day turns to night, fall to winter, young to old, hot to cold, they are met with resistance and regret. It always seems that good things are ruined by bad as evil lurks in the shadow of optimism. We try to entertain our lives, continuously reminiscing about joyful times as we cry at the funerals of our own hopes and dreams. For many, the good times are too distant a memory. With this in mind, we walk on with our lives, trying desperately to create newfound joy. It is now that we must realize that storms do happen and lingering among us is Yang appended to Yin. What you think you know is about to change.

Throughout my life I always had a desire, this thing lingering in me, an itching like feeling to be more than what I was. I never understood it, and as far as I could tell no-one else around me seemed to care about it either. If other people were feeling it too, they certainly didn't show it. I've done many things in my life, and we'll discuss that later. For now, just know that every venture I went on always ended the same. I'd get really good at what I was doing, and then out of nowhere, something happened and that was the end of that.

A couple of decades later, I discovered that the universe is governed by laws. I'm not talking about judicial laws, I'm talking about laws that govern how things work and why things are the way they are. The first example told to me was the law of electricity. No-one really knows what electricity is, we just know how to use it. We also know that if we use it wrong, it can kill us. This got my attention and my mind pondering. It was during my interest in these laws that I stumbled across an age-old Chinese philosophy, Yin and Yang. The well-known iconic black and white ball which insists one cannot exist without the other, and that opposites attract.

I thought about this for a couple of years. Now that may seem like a long time, however it was instrumental to my new way of thinking and living. You will find that throughout this book you will see many examples of what I'm about to share with you. I encourage that when you discover them, you read and deliberate upon them. Then choose wisely how to apply them.

Yin and Yang may seem evident to you, and you may say "well yeah, of course" but I really truly want you to think about this. For every yes there must be a no. For many people the no's hold a heavy burden. For every cold day there's a warm day. Every winter has a summer, and every night has a day. What goes up must come down, and what goes in must come out.

I was, and still am so intrigued by this and somehow, every time I was getting good at something, it was taken away from me... and it surprised me every time. I was yet to understand that for every good there is bad, its law. So, with that notion I choose to use the age-old philosophy to help you discover your light amongst your darkness.

HOW I CAME TO WRITE
THIS BOOK

A s we make choices, we tend to use our own personal experiences, other people's experiences, and our internal gut feelings to make them. Since the day we were born we've stored our ideas, philosophies, and opinions deep in our minds. We use our senses to discover new things, and our reactions to remember them. The first time a kid touches a hot stove, it demonstrates this to be true. The smell of stinky feet is another prime example. Yet, when we store our opinions away and fail to grasp the full scoop of our reactions. If I were to buy a new pair of shoes and ask that you smell them, they wouldn't smell bad, but still you'd probably knock the shoe away from me. Our minds are full of filtered experiences, and many of them come from the people we hold close to us. My grandmother has been telling me all my life "it's too risky to invest money", and so I didn't for over thirty years. I used her experiences and advice as my own personal experience. Without realizing it, most of us do this.

To accurately understand how I came to write this book I am going to take you on a journey through my life. This isn't so that I can brag, and to be honest there's not much to brag about. It is my hope that by going through my life's journey, that you reflect on your own journey so far and relate to the ideas shared in this book.

My relation to my home town is one of uniqueness. I was a military kid born in Germany. By age three my parents had divorced. My mother, sister, and I moved to England to live with my grandmother. My grandmother was born and bred in Glasgow, Scotland and moved to England with her father during World War II. Many Scot's moved to England for employment by British Steel, one of Europe's biggest steel providers at the time. I was an American, born in Germany, living in England, in a Scottish-dominant town. Talk about cultural diversity. I was all types of confused.

I went to school in England and like many kids, I hated school. There were some good times such as field trips and making some friends, however for the most part I couldn't stand it. Around age seven I had this self-awareness that I thought differently than others and that my calling was to be on the big stage. My break came when I was asked to play one of the three kings in the Nativity play. I was on stage, playing a major role and people applauded me. It felt great. It was around that same time that I started to get bullied. It wasn't just getting called names. I lived no further than 500ft away from school and I couldn't walk home alone without getting beat up.

Around age nine, my mother pulled me out of school for a while and I went to her place of work. My mother had about seven jobs, some volunteer and others paid. She worked at a youth center, advising pregnant teenagers, troubled youth who were caught up in the jail system, disabled, and drug addicted teens. From an early age I was exposed to all types of people. These teens were friendly, helpful, kind, and loving to me. It seemed as if they desired acceptance as much as I did. Even after I went back to school a couple months later, I'd still go to my mother's work after final bell. I was intrigued by these teens' life stories and discovered hope in the eyes of the disheartened. It was hard not to see my mother since she worked so much but I took pride in knowing she volunteered her time to help those who needed it most.

At school my concentration level was zero as I was distracted by being bullied. My mother enrolled me in Karate. This was part self-defense and part self-confidence building. During Karate I enjoyed being in the circle, all eyes on me, while we tested our new skills on each other. Very quickly I ranked up and before I knew it I was in both the youth and adult classes. Not many kids could say they were fighting adults. I was good, better than good, I was becoming the best. My internal desire to be on the big stage drove me to practice around the clock so that I would be noticed. Throughout that same period, I was also taking swimming lessons but I didn't care for that too much and had no real desire to be athletic since I was told I had asthma from an early age. Convinced of my asthmatic condition, I used this excuse to not attempt any physical activity what-so-ever, except karate. As I was at the peak of my karate sphere, the family car broke down and we couldn't afford to fix it. I wasn't going to allow my mother to waste money on taxis, or her time waiting around for me for two hours, and anyway that would cut into my favorite television show at the time, so I quit.

When I moved to high school, the bullying died down slightly. It wasn't fully gone, but manageable. I made new friends and was optimistic about the future. I came home from school one night and saw my Grandmother practicing this weird dancing, so as eleven olds do, I made fun of her. The following Monday my Grandmother grabbed me by the ear and dragged me along to line dancing. I realized very quickly that there were other kids my age there, and I might be able to sneak some beer here and there too. What I didn't realize was that my grandmother was going to grab me once again by the ear and onto the dance floor to learn a dance that was being taught. To everyone's surprise, especially my own, I was good at it. I wasn't just good, I was great and quickly becoming the best. A few months later I went to another line dance instructor's class. For the sake of privacy, I will call him Steve. I enjoyed watching Steve dance as his feet floated through the air and glided along the floor. I practiced every day to dance just like Steve. A couple more months went by and Steve handed me the mic. He wanted me to teach a line dance to his class. I was 12 years old, and everyone was looking at me. I'd been practicing for this day for over a year. I got up and taught the best dance there was. It wasn't long until I was teaching each week in Steve's class. I wasn't getting paid, and I didn't care. I was in the spot light and having fun.

When it rains, it pours. Everyone's heard that expression, and they always view it in a negative light. I've come to learn that when good things happen, they too can also all happen at once. My Monday, Tuesday and occasional Friday and Saturday nights were now dedicated to dancing. I endured much mockery at school about my line dancing, even by some teachers, but what did I care? I was on stage weekly. Around this time in my life, I was on the school bus heading to school. There was a kid I had a run in with the previous week on the back of the bus and he had a guitar. I had made a 'your momma' joke to him in the school café not realizing his mother had just passed away after losing her battle with cancer, so I couldn't blame him for being upset with me. He was talking to some kids on the bus saying he's looking for a guitarist for a band he's trying to start. Now I knew about three chords and was willing to give anything a shot, so I said I'd jam with him. He was skeptical given the recent encounter we had, but too was optimistic in his search for the stage. I invited the drummer and base player over to my house for our first practice. This practice came as a surprise to my family, in fact the whole street was surprised. Before we practiced there was something I always wanted to do. So, I hopped behind the drum set and started banging away. The bass player, who was the kid on the back of the bus, asked me how long I'd been playing drums for. I told him for about ten seconds and then something happened. He showed me a basic beat and I picked up on it quick. He told me I was going to be his drummer, and that's how we formed a band. He loaned me this little drum kit and instructed me to practice. To the amusement of the whole neighborhood, I practiced every single day, hours upon hours, listening to all types of music and trying to mimic the beat.

Six months later, after practicing twice a week as a band, the bass player did something that I did not agree to and in fact objected to vigorously. His dad knew a music producer who was willing to come and help us for a few hours for free. I didn't want no producer telling me how to play the drums, nor telling us how we should play our music. We turned up to rehearsal at the local music studio, and there the producer was. Our bass player had gone behind my back and got him to come down anyway. We were already there, and had parted with some money for the practice room, so I might as well just get this over and done with. We had four original songs and spent about an hour breaking down each one. After about an hour I soon learned that the producer wasn't there to show us how to play, he was there to show us how to mold together as musicians.

We alternated practices from the studio to my family's garage. The day after the producer was with us, we practiced in my garage and something strange happened. After we had practiced a couple of songs, we opened up the garage door to go get some drinks and there was a little gathering outside. One of the ladies said, "We don't know what happened to you guys, but you guys are good". This gave us a new-found belief, and so we went knocking on doors. We knocked on every single bar and pub's door within a fifty-mile radius, hoping to land some gigs. No-one would book us without a demo. The bass player's dad fronted the money and we went into the studio and recorded our four songs. We went back knocking on doors and landed our first gig. We got paid about $20 bucks for our first gig, and we were dreadful. We continued hustle and bust our backsides and our efforts soon paid off. We obtained frequent gigs, and had a little following going.

The hustle that came with the band gave me new confidence and so I grabbed onto an open opportunity and began teaching line dancing to my own class. The first few weeks were hard, however after a short few months I had a following and was gaining a name for myself at age 13. If I wasn't practicing drums or practicing with the band, I was practicing line dancing. My whole week consisted of a strict routine of practice and performance. And to be honest, at age 13 I was making great money. Very quickly my dream of being on stage was a reality, and I loved every second of it. Every waking moment my thoughts consisted of the next move, my next objective, and how I was going to overcome the next hurdle. I had [have] this burning fire in me that always wanted to push me to greater achievements. Understanding what this fire was is what proved to be difficult.

When I turned 15, and was about to leave high school, the band had a meeting, and we decided to split up. I wanted to join the army, and the others had ambitions they wanted to chase. At the same time, I gave up line dancing. I figured after everything I'd been through, I had my life figured out and was on the track to greatness. I only went to school to take my finals and never went back for the results. It turned out I couldn't join the British army without becoming a British citizen. They wanted me to test for citizenship, wait for results, and all this other stuff that quite frankly I was not interested in. I wanted to join the army for so long, I was even enrolled in the British army cadet program, and yet this test was a detrimental blow to my hyped-up psyche. So, I ended up working in a food factory. That burning desire to go and do more was always with me, lighting me up. As a standard line-worker in the factory, I started volunteering for overtime. Then I volunteered on my weekends. Any course that came up, I jumped on it. I was reliable, hardworking, people liked me, and the next thing I knew I was getting promoted within months over people who had been there for years. My clothes were always ironed and creased, I showed up early and left late daily and was making more money than I knew what to do with, so I did the next best thing, I spent it all. I worked at the factory for a couple years, and then one day, without notice or anything lined up for myself, I quit. I wanted adventure, I wanted to enjoy myself, and I wanted control of my life. There had to be something bigger and better.

Turns out that all that waited for me were bills with no income to pay them. I ended up taking a stroll to a local delivery company, and became a delivery driver. I made decent money, but it wasn't anything I was used to before that. My inner fire was running out of fuel, and I found a new love... soccer. Not playing, watching. I was in the bar all day and night drinking my life away. Started showing up late to work, not caring about much or what was happening to me. I ended up losing my job and my house as I couldn't afford rent. I found myself in a hole and saw no light. Ironically, I found money to keep going to the bar and eventually that's all I could think about.

At 20 years old, I walked into my mother's house after an afternoon session at the bar and found myself in what I can only describe as an intervention. I was told that I was drinking my life away and that I should try joining the American armed forces. I wanted nothing to do with this and stormed off back to the bar. But something was still burning inside me. I remembered how I gave up all hope of joining the British army and how upset I was that my dreams seemed to be stolen away from me.

A few weeks later, I went online and started doing some research. I was slowly becoming obsessed with the idea of joining the United States Air Force. I made a phone call and a few weeks later I found myself on an Air Force base taking the ASVAB. My excitement and overconfidence were soon to be shunned. A couple of weeks later I received my results. Now I'm not stupid, nor dumb, however this was my first Americanized test I'd ever taken, so if Johnny walks into a shop with ten dimes and I don't know what a dime was, then how am I supposed to know what change he should receive? After failing to meet the minimal requirements of the ASVAB, that fire inside me burned brighter. I was determined that I would join the United States Air Force. Another few weeks went by, and there I found myself taking the ASVAB again. This time, when the results came in, I missed the Air Force cut off by one point, however had enough to join the Army. Now, with the Iraq war in full swing, this is not what my family wanted me to do. I found myself a private math teacher and studied math. I figured if I could bump my score up in one portion, I'd have enough to join the Air Force. Bingo, it worked. My third attempt at the ASVAB and I was in.

At 25 years old my son Hance, was born and shortly after I wound up in Iraq for a year. Upon returning from Iraq, I was greeted with divorce papers from my first wife. This wasn't an easy divorce by any means and drained my mental facility down to zero. It was at the tail end of this divorce that I met my second wife. I deployed shortly after meeting her, and upon arrival home we were married. A couple years later we were sitting down having a discussion where she asked me" what's my end game?" She wanted to know my overall goal in life. Now by this time I was pretty self-confident, had a good career, and knew what the one major goal in my life was. I told her. Now I choose not to share my life goals with many people, and throughout this book you too may choose to end up not sharing your goals. After some deep thinking, she turned to me and said,

"You know what scares me is that if anyone could do it, I believe it's you". Now her ambitions were high, however there is no cover for the height of my goals. I knew this was the beginning of the end of our relationship as our paths were not meant to stay straight nor together. Simultaneously, I was going through unexpected, unfounded hardship at work and that's when depression hit me. I'm not sure if it was just me feeling sorry for myself, or if it was actual depression. I do know this, three years later is a long time to come out of a state in which there seemed to be no end in sight. Throughout this time, I hid my confusion, sadness, and anger in the bottom of a bottle. I gained thirty pounds, neglected my self-interest, and ran away from myself. I did manage to somehow marry my wonderful wife, Stephanie and we ended up renting a nice little family home. It was here were the unexpected happened.

I don't know why things happen when they happen, I just know they do. And in many cases, it always seems to be at the right time. Whilst I was in the height of my depression, drinking daily, and barely keeping my head above water, what I can only describe as a God send happened to me. Each night I'd take a walk around the corner to the mail box to receive mail. We were still receiving mail from the old tenants, so I took a pen with me and would write "NATA", Not At This Address, on the mail and would slip it back in for return. One particular evening, whilst retrieving the mail, there was a magazine titled 'Success' in my mail box. Now I know we didn't order magazines and the addressee's name confirmed that. I looked over both my shoulders and did something extremely immoral. I slipped the magazine under my shirt and ran home. Now it was late in the evening, I had an early wake up time, but with a title like success, I wanted to know more. I flipped through the pages, reading the bold headlines, discovering what the magazine was about. Centerfold there laid a Compact Disk. I ripped the disk out, set it by my car keys and went to bed. Early the next morning on the way to work I listened to this CD. Tracks one to three were okay and were more background noise than anything, but then it happened. Track four came on and my life was about to change. Track four was an extract from a seminar conducted by Jim Rohn. At the time I didn't even know what a seminar was, let alone the ideas this gentleman was about to share with me. I was so excited after hearing these twenty minutes that I couldn't wait to finish work so that I could hear it again. I got home and listened to it yet another time. I became so obsessed with what he was saying that I gathered all his stuff and went on a binge. The binge has not ended and never will. I never knew Jim personally, but I do truly owe him a huge thank you for introducing me to personal development.

After a few years of reading, listening, and obtaining all these personal development ideas, I soon realized that just like me, many people around me had never heard of personal development or understood it to its entire extent. Many people write this off as "motivational speaking", however personal development is way more than motivation. Anyway, there is only one type of motivation and that's self-motivation. To think that anyone else can motivate you is like thinking you can lose weight if someone else diets for you.

I was talking with a co-worker about my wife's pregnancy, and the challenges that arise from this, such as how will I afford to feed my family? How can I be the role-model my child deserves? Where will this extra money for daycare come from? In passing I said "She's pregnant and I'm screwed". This hit home very quickly. I wonder how many people in the world have fears about daily challenges with no answers. I wondered if only they knew what I knew, I mean I had all this personal development stuff and at least I had a jump start for the search to all my questions.

Almost two years later, I still wonder how many people are struggling with the daily ins and outs of life, and why they don't have the answers they desperately seek. Hence, I decided to bring this book to you, so you too can begin your transformation and become the person you've always dreamed of.

THE "FUN" HERD EFFECT

With summer in full swing, billboards, television commercials, flyers and newspapers all tell us how summer should be spent. Drink in hand, water in the background, sunshades reflecting the summer light seem to reflect accurately how we should be spending our summer days. The marketing behind this typical scenario has most people reaching deep into their pockets and spending money on unrealistic expectations of fun in the sun. However most will drain their bank accounts aiming at this ideal image. The mall is full of people throwing away dollar bills in the millions. Airports become suction tunnels. Disney World continues to thrive on family fun. The beaches erect sunbrellas reaching for miles. River beds fill with cellphones of innocents tubing in the day's sun rays. City buildings are glowing, radiating the summer sun. Popsicle, snow cones, and ice tea fill the hands of millions, all reaching for the ideal summer. All it takes is for each person to either look left or right to realize that what they are doing is the same as most others. Even the person who they exclaim to dislike happens to be doing the exact same thing as them. Once again summer has announced itself. The herd has arrived, and it has expectations.

THE MENTAL MIRROR

As we begin our journey, I find myself sitting here pondering life, its issues and hacks. As with everything, the only way we will truly understand what is going on for us and around us is through self reflection. This doesn't *yet* mean sitting down with a pen and paper and writing anything down, or meditation in the early morning. This simply means that we should place on our mental running shoes and allow our minds to start jogging, pondering the scenic views.

With my shoes tied, I recollect summer which passed on by like poop through a goose. Summer seems recent yet a distant memory. I'm sure, as with most, summer was filled with enjoyment, fun, laughter and quite frankly was fantastic. River trips accompanied by a few cold ones were a must. Back yard get togethers seemed an everyday occurrence. Grilled flavored smoke filled the suburbs of the city. Sing-a-long music replaced bird chirping in every neighborhood. Laughter projected into the streets as silliness occupied the man holding a spatula in one hand and a beer in another. All in all, summer was a feel-good time. Most evenings, dusk drew upon us replacing the blazing sun with moonlight, lighting up the starlit sky as if Sir David

Attenborough was commentating on nature's beauty. Caught up in the ideal setting, giggling with silliness, company departed. Taking full advantage of the "Hollywood"-like setting, the wife and I romanced into the early hours. It was, and to this day, still is pleasant and comforting knowing each other would fall asleep in one another's arms. The summer of 69 seemed to have a competitor.

BUYER'S REMORSE

J ust like the man who cheated on his wife, or the kid who stole money from his parents. A sickening, faint feeling shrivels through the body upon instant completion. The mind becomes foggy, hands sweat, nerves twitching. Guilt and remorse now become the frontal vortex of the soul. Summer fun has ridden its course, and now it's time to pay.

Gazing through the window observing the drip of each leaf layer on the ground. Hearing the crisp scatter of golden leaves lay motionless waiting for a breeze to mar them along. My nose was alerted by the smell of pumpkin spice and apple flavor scents filling each room. Creepy faces appear on neighborhood doorsteps in the form of fruit. Holiday festive's creep among the masses. A steady realization hits that autumn has knocked on the door. Driving to work is more chaotic than usual. A look out of the drizzled-smeared car window reveals town centers and malls are quieter. Music played from the car radio becomes drowned by the noise of kids screaming from behind the fences of their schools. A picture paints a thousand words as children giggle play hop scotch on chalked sidewalks.

THE ITCHING FEELING

Heaven seems only to exist to the man who lives in hell. Brightness is golden for the man living in the dark. Change is welcomed only by those suffering. Every transition in form has a process, and each and everyone of us realizes the change at different points. To some it may be the drop in temperature, others may be the overcast of clouds, and some may be the actual date on the calendar. Nether less, all will notice at some point, and will itch with rashes of past memory's rather than desire of new changes.

Days seem longer yet the light of day is shorter. Each morning the alarm clock screams louder and louder. Irritation flows through the bones. Family and friends seem engagingly intrusive in personal matters. Neighbors ring the doorbell daily asking to borrow tools that they still have a hold of. An influx of neighborhood dogs has amassed, barking the cold right out of the air. It seems the postal man awakes earlier, ringing the doorbell at new founds of morning. Even though the year is only two thirds away through, one must awake that the year has been a-miss and yet seemingly flew on by.

The waist line is tight from all the delicious grub eaten. The missus is blatantly unhappy, even after remembering the pumpkin latte. Flashbacks of childhood spark the mind while grounded at work. The only productive exercise seems to be eyeballing the slow-moving clock on the wall.

Questions start to appear amidst the daydreams. What direction in life is one going? Where is that degree I swear to get? How did the dealership talk me into a high-payment car? The 'debt consolidation loan' that took all hard to pay small loans and placed them into one big hard to pay loan. The vacation that was talked about all summer yet will never see the light of day. The store credit cards because that new swimming pool, grill, and nightstand all 'needed' to be replaced. How come one or two divorces didn't teach me anything? Clothes worn are the same old combinations. Bank account is empty. The missus wants you to get a "better paid" job. At work, the boss wants to enhance that "Monday" feeling by having a few choice words to share. This only leads to division in the workplace. Traffic on the freeway is like a parking lot. Radio news echoes the sounds of depression. The phone is blowing up from unknown numbers, which internally you know are creditors. That ten percent chance of rain becomes hazard warnings, overflowing drain systems ensuring roads are fit for the national swimming team.

WHEN IT HITS

F un times, buyers' remorse, itching for diversity of change all add up to a harsh reality. The mental jog should now be in full sprint. The only stopping point is running straight into a brick wall. Before you hit that wall, one last ill action has to be completed. Whatever the action may be, it will be the biggest regret of the attitude one's ever had.

Drenched, as you take the first few steps into your home, rings of silence mist the air. You place dishes into the dishwasher, laundry thrown into the dishwasher, floors mopped, cleaning the dirt and rain you dragged in. The missus comes home overly excited, yet mesmerizingly emotional. A weird combination. But there isn't anything new, right?!! Trouble shooting in your mind, the list is checked off. Ladies' week? No. Anniversary? No. Birthday? No. Dinner date? No. Friends coming over? No. Maybe, just maybe she hit the lottery. Nah, she would have tweeted that by now. Focusing on chores, you stare at the cold brew turn not so cold. She hands you something. "It can hold on"!! You exclaim. Now she's edgy, you're upset. You want to relax and she wants you to read this 'dumb note'. Chores done;

you eventually get to this ever so important note. Your mind is now racing. Awareness becomes six senses like. She's been in the bathroom longer than usual. You read this note over and over again, however the words seem to just mesh. A sick tightening tension stiffens the whole body. That cold brew is as distant as summer. Every chick flick you ever watched flashes through your mind like a strike of lightning. In the corner of your eye lay unpaid bills. Staring in your direction with a hammer fist stands a picture of you and your missus. Family values, religious preaching, and other people's perception of you all seem to matter a great deal right now. The spare bedroom that you and your boys watched the game in has suddenly disappeared. The missus, of course, the missus!! You run to the bathroom, however it's locked. Like SWAT breeching a house you bang on the door loudly. Trap door type, the door creeks open. Excited emotional transmissions of her are confusing you. The dumb note wasn't that dumb. Your reactions were unjust. You flash back to moments earlier where chores seemed to be the biggest deal and your drink was your reward for a day of unsettling and rubble. Resembling puss-in-boots, she stares you in the eyes. She murmurs the words and reality kicks in; SHE'S PREGNANT AND YOU'RE SCREWED.

Nothing makes sense. Upsetting your pregnant missus by freaking out over a note is incomprehensible. Why would you do such a thing? Why couldn't that be the one time you listened? Selfish, only thinking about yourself! That's not how you usually treat a lady. As you stare into the ever-dimmed ceiling light for answers. Hearts racing. Thoughts negatively flow. How are you going to survive? Bank statements reflect immediate regret. That twenty in your wallet seems increasingly small. The back yard seems to have grown over the last hour, needing maintenance. Your place of work is laying off personnel, and you think you're on the chopping block. That proud, strong fearless person everyone watched, laughed with and trusted over the summer is now a miniscule, fearful man that family and friends are now leaning on for answers.

AND THERE YOU HAVE IT

W hen you seem to be on top of the world, the world has a unique way of jerking you to the knees, humbling the most heartful soul. I feel this is important as no one is susceptible to bad comings or changes. Many times, we have heard, it's not what happens that matters, it's what we do about it that counts. Too many times we sit back and wish we'd never done a certain thing or said a certain statement. Education of the mind and soul is crucial to a successful life, and where best to start than in the past? If something worked, do more of it, if something failed, eliminate doing that, and if you did or said something years ago, or a maar ten minutes ago that makes your body and soul cringe, don't repeat.

TRUTH BE TOLD

A family isn't made up of one person, a thousand dollars has 100,000 cents, a work force has more than one employee, and a house has more than one brick. We have a tendency to overthink, overreact, and hold on to thoughts that should be let go. When we mess up, think negatively, or upset someone we didn't want to upset, that icky sickening feeling seems to linger within us. Realize that we think hundreds and thousands of thoughts a day. We also say many things in a short time frame. We mess up, and it's okay. Sometimes it takes a simple apology to surpass action. Other times it takes many years. No matter the case, forgive yourself, make mental (and physical) note of the situation leading up to, and the actual action itself and learn from it. Reading the previous dialogue might have placed you in that lingering of guilt. You might feel slightly sick and frustrated, recalling a similar scenario that you have found yourself in. Rest assured, you are not alone. The previous dialogue happened to me. I intentionally left parts out because they are personal. Placing myself back into that moment and mindset made my hands sweaty, and my stomach sick.

WHAT YOU NEEDED
TO HEAR

The truth hurts, yet the truth will set you free. Play with that in your mind for a bit. You don't know me, and I don't know you. Yet, the words that you're reading speak right to you. This is good. This means that as much pain as there is in the world, freedom shall be right behind its doors. I am grateful for pain and I suggest you be too. I am grateful for what pain represents. In our darkest hours, this is where we find the testament to our will and courage. We either choose to lay down or continue our daily grind and routine in which we keep faith that it shall prevail. When my ex-wife left me, I decided to lay down. I chose to drink instead of continuing. I gained weight, and my expertise was no longer of value. Now-a-days, I invite my darkest hour to meet me. Pain represents the wall which we must break to achieve greatness. The Berlin Wall, West Germany, is a physical representation of this. Today, I urge you to start being grateful for pain.

I don't claim to have all the answers. I search for answers to life just as many of you do. I make it my daily pleasure to search for answers. I don't believe I will ever truly find them. If I do find answers, my belief is that I may never truly understand them.

This is okay with me as it gives me something to keep working towards. The why has always got to be bigger than the task at hand and searching for life's answers is my why. I do believe I have garnished some invaluable knowledge. I treat the mind as I would a glass of water. It is not my concern if the glass is half empty or full, nor do I care. I care for the know that if I empty my glass, I can place more water into it. Therefore, if I share my knowledge, not only do I see the fruits of my labor within you. I get to fill my mind with more knowledge. I have now created space for more ideas and wisdom. I will never lose track of the knowledge I've emptied out. I hope that your success stories will be my daily reminder of what is possible and that my words act as spilled water, watering dried out flower's.

It is with all faith, sincerity, and honesty that I share with you life's little gifts. Once applied, these gifts can drastically turn your life around. I am not someone who is going to tell you that the ideas in this book are easy. I will say that every single one of them is SIMPLE.

CHAOS THEORY

C ommonly known as the butterfly effect, Murphy's laws, or in keeping it simple, YIN, states that toughness, hardship, pain, all seem to happen at once. Whatever it is you've heard this to be called realize this; Since the beginning of mankind, when things go wrong, they go very wrong. Ever wake up, stub your toe, trip in the dark, cut yourself shaving, and the day speeds downhill? Traffic is backing up. Every traffic light is red. You spilled your coffee. Rip your shirt. Late to work. Computer doesn't work. The client doesn't show. Are you starting to relate? There is so much confusion and happening all in a short period, and for most, all in one day. It is here where suppositions are born. The exact same things may happen another day, the only difference is you did not stub your toe, and it is marked as a good day. You are not focused on the one event that started the day off. This causes people to wear lucky boxers, have a favorite toothbrush, touch the 'lucky' ornament three times before leaving the door, which none will help you apart from a shift in thought.

A mother is driving home from the grocery store, when suddenly her vehicle is struck by another. Emergency services on scene, insurance company wanting to appraise the damage, and the family blowing up the phone asking her where-abouts. At this point one may confuse the car crash and all its immediate madness, and perceive time as stopping. Yet the truth couldn't be any further. The mother's means of transportation have been taken away, a couple of days of work have to be missed, and the bills still have to be paid. We hear it all the time, as people recollect a memory. "Time stood still" they would say. And then continue with the chaotic aftermath of their story.

Just when we think time has stopped, it turns out that the roller-coaster of life has taken that split second pause at the top. The one that allows you to take that deep breath in and as you start to think you may be stuck, all of a sudden it speeds downhill. We should really analyze this for its true value. The harder a ball is dropped, the higher it goes. The faster we roll downhill, the further uphill the momentum will take us. We must all go downhill and reach the bottom before heading up. Each moment you feel time has paused, brace yourself. The turbulence of life is about to shake things up.

We all have bad days, and this book won't stop a bad day from happening. What it will do is guide and show you simple and effective ways to deal with your shortcomings. More so than ever bad days, hard comings, being wronged by, scammed, disliked, have never been so important to deal with.

INK TO PAPER

There comes a point at which each of us must realize that we cannot trust our memory. It doesn't matter if you have a photographic memory, or you can't even remember your second cousin's name. The more information we have, the less likely we are to remember it all. At one point or another we've all said "I wish I had written that down". Let's start our daily change with this simple task...start writing. Write down all the information you wish to use later. Be the person to whom others seek advice because they know if you don't remember it, you'll have it written down. You will seem smarter, sound smarter, and all in all be a smarter person. Now who wouldn't want that as a reputation? You can be that 'person' you've always envied. The one who always seems to have a wealth of knowledge, and just seems so smart while everyone else stares in ear at their wisdom.

With that in mind I advise you at this point to start taking notes. All in one day I heard a few life-changing tips. Number one: If you want to be like the top five percent, walk away from the 95%. Number two: If a good book is recommended, don't be like the 95% and not buy it. Stand out from others and immediately purchase the book. Number three: Take notes (preferably in some sort of journal). When I listened to this all I immediately went to the bookstore and brought the very book that was recommended. Right away I felt myself breaking away from the 95%.

REMEMBERING

Most of us say we are close to others. I know a few years ago I would claim I was close to all my friends, family, and work colleagues. It wasn't until I was asked a question about a certain work colleague which I couldn't answer that I realized that I wasn't as close as I thought I was. I started to look at all my relationships and question my closeness to everyone. I started with myself then I moved out to my wife, my son, my mother, sister, extended family, friends, and then co-workers. It sounds bizarre, however we spend the majority of our time with other people, so why not get close to them? Simple things like learning full names, children's names, where they live, what school people went to. This doesn't have to be a complex exercise. What this will do is open doors that have never seen the light of day. This lets others know you care. It shows your sharpness, shows your wiliness to be on top of your game, shows your ability to show compassion with others, shows others your character is above average. Ever met someone for a few moments, then years later you see that same person again and they ask how your wife is doing by name? Remember how impressed you were? You can do that. You can show the ability to communicate a closeness with each person you meet. If you are like me and suck at remembering names, keep a small book, or some sort of file of everyone you know and have met. It takes a little time time. However, when you next speak to that person you can recall little things like names and big things like what was discussed the last time you both spoke. You don't have to have a large memory bank. Learn these little tricks that keep you sharp and on point. Note, closeness is not about how close you feel others are to you. It's the chain for the bridge in each relationship. Closeness is about how close you are to other people. Have your friends' kids be excited to come to your house. Have them say "Wow, I can't wait to go over. He remembers everything we like". Have your friends say over a couple of cocktails, "How do you remember all this?" Keep notes, keep track, and study all you meet. You never know who you might run into, or where you might find yourself later in life. Impress others for yourself, don't impress yourself for others. Remember simple things such as favorite foods, or favorite songs. These will go a long way. Keep track of your likes and dislikes. Impress even your family members and be that role model. Stand out from others, and remember NEVER trust your memory. Since cavemen, the human race has been scribing thoughts and observations. Being that on walls with stone, trees with a sharp object, or pen to paper. We remember our history, our lessons, our roots by scribing them. I continue to suggest you do the same.

BECAUSE OTHERS HAVE
SAID SO...

I find it ironic that the very people who tell us what we can and can't do things are the same people that if we choose to ignore, we end up surpassing. You see I was made to believe in high school that I was dyslexic. This drastically changed my life goals. I went from wanting to be a lawyer to joining the armed forces. One involved reading a lot and the other not so much. Many years later I'm listening to some guy tell me something completely different. Of course I was going to buy the recommended book. I was so intrigued by the book I purchased that I managed to read it in three hours. After reading it I immediately was blowing up all my friends' phones. I wouldn't stop talking about this book to my wife. I just couldn't shut up about this book.

As I was recalling the book to a friend of mine, I couldn't remember some key points. It was then that I realized my first mistake. I hadn't taken notes. I quickly found myself back in the book store buying myself a journal. The same day I re-read the book and took notes. I will not make this mistake again. Each book I read I take notes. I philosophize my own interpretations and keep notes. I view my journal as I view my life; a blank piece of paper. Whatever I write about it can, if I choose, become reality. I recommend taking notes and being in a mindset of optimism and enthusiasm as we venture over the course of this book. Words are powerful, especially when written down. Not quite sure of this, just think of America's founding document, the United States Constitution.

BETWEEN THE LINES

YOU are going to learn new ideas on how to re-gain control over yourself and your thoughts. As you read, I urge you to look between the lines. It's between the lines that you will find the answers you are seeking. Use this book to guide you through your quest as you lunge deep into your own personal train of thought. Let this book walk you through the next few days, weeks, months, and years. Allow the ideas to speak to you directly, as if I were giving you one-on-one advice. Feel the hand of acceptance lean you towards a new way of thinking. Let the words jump out and place themselves on your mental shelf of prized possessions.

PERSONAL
DEVELOPMENT

P ersonal development is absolutely vital for success and for you to shine. You must change the small things. I was watching a soccer game the other day, and at half time, the team I wanted to win was losing, and losing badly. The second half came and I saw a couple of players had been substituted. The team went on to win that match, and at full team I smirked. My friend asked "what's the smirk for?" "that's it" I replied, "you never see a soccer manager change the whole team because they are losing, they change one or two things". It's the same with personal development. Chances are you don't have to change a whole lot. You just have to change a few small things to impact the end game. You may have to change everything, that is possible, and if that is the case I suggest you start right away. I recommend starting off with appearance. I recall one evening, my wife and I were watching the movie, Intern. An older gentleman applies for an internship at a new fashion company which is located in the gentleman's old line of work where he used to be the boss. Of course, set in the modern era, the fashion company has work ethics which I can only describe as what working for Google or Facebook would be like. Own clothes, modern technology, the full works. Well, the gentleman competes against younger individuals for this job. Near the end of the movie...the Gentleman has influenced the younger staff members. He influenced them by first...suit and tie, then a briefcase, clean shaven, and then mannerisms; what I refer to as gentlemanlike. It was a friendly reminder to me of a few things. It reminded me that the foundations have not changed, that chivalry has not died, and that being different will always set you apart from the crowd, and in-turn will eventually be the example.

...HAPPY WITH OTHERS

M any people make the mistake of buying someone else's program for happiness. Even worse, they claim it to be theirs. Elvis Presley, the king of rock, was known for buying Cadillacs for random consumers. You may say, 'well yeah, I'd do the same if I had his money.' Elvis's nice gesture just never seemed to be enough for him. Many close to him relayed his dissatisfaction with life, mental depression, and lack of love from one to another. Actor Jim Carrey is known for saying "I wish everyone had fame and fortune so they would realize happiness is not found there". You must step out of your comfort zone. Be broke for a while. Be broke in mind, soul, and money. Lose some 'friends', have some sleepless nights. Most people don't and won't understand this. They don't and won't understand what you're doing, why you're acting 'different'. They'll disown you. If the grass is greener on the other, stop staring. Stop comparing. Stop complaining and start watering the grass you are standing on. Never regret a day in your life; good days give happiness, bad days give experience, worst days give lessons, and the best days give memories. Be grateful for others. Love seeing others succeed. Life is a journey, not a competition. Sometimes all we can do is accept what is, let go of what was, and have faith in what will be. Follow your heart, however, take your brain with you. As you awaken you will come to understand that the journey to love isn't about finding 'the one'. The journey is about becoming 'the one'. Happiness is a choice. When you can't control what's happening, challenge yourself to control the way you respond to what's happening. That is where the power is. Stop worrying, change negative thinking, forgive. Forgiveness heals the soul, cures depression, and increases good health. "Forgiveness is not forgetting. Forgiveness is the other side of gratitude. Gratitude is a positive response to benefits, whilst forgiveness is a positive response to harm" ... 'Why good things happen to good people, Stephen Post Ph.D., and Jill Neimark.' Be grateful. Start the morning off by writing down things you are grateful for. I'd recommend a page in that journal. This does wonders for the mental faculties. Take part in meaningful activities. Giving back, spending time with loved ones, and generally delivering thankfulness is the soul's love for the human mind which shows gratefulness in all aspects of one's life. Enjoy the simple pleasures. Life gets really expensive with all these theme parks, restaurants, and kids' activities. Simplify the chaos. Buy a soccer ball and go to a field and kick the ball around. Take a walk if you have a dog. A perfect opportunity for valuable family time. Enjoy the giggles of your child{ren} and listen to their tears of need. Decorate for the holidays as a family, and help your family make decorations, then flaunt them proudly. Lastly, but mainly, write your goals down. This is important. Wonder why you're walking around feeling lost and hopeless, in a dead-end job, and for some no job at all? Wonder why luck seems to skip you? It's because you're walking around hoping and praying. Faith is important, yet you still have to provide a prayer and say a wish for it to come true. Writing down your goals gives you a sense of direction, and also it introduces you to new ways of thinking and doing which equals accomplishment. Have a goal list and make it number one to be happy. Work on yourself, by yourself, for yourself. We either make ourselves miserable, or we make ourselves strong and happy. Either way the amount of work is the same.

Relationships take work, and many of us have discovered it. The amount of work you put in will come back tenfold. It's just the way it works. I choose not to try and understand this. Instead, I dedicate my time to the application of personal development. I find the smiles of many around me fill me with joy. I most certainly retain that the laughter of my child is the warmest feeling I've ever experienced. Why? Who knows and who cares? It just is. The relationship I have with my wife will transcribe over to how your child views relationships. Respect and humility shape the overall character of a successful individual. U2 once sang "If you want to kiss the sky, better learn how to kneel". Getting it wrong is a major part of our lives. Be humble, say you're sorry, and press forward. I do find it intriguing though, that no matter how much one works on themselves, the need and desire for a partner lingers. To some, the relationship with their child satisfies this need. Others say marriage does it justice. Many find both combined to fill their emptiness with companionship. In France they don't say 'I miss you'. Instead they say 'Tu Me Manqué' which translates to 'you are missing from me'. How beautiful.

EDUCATIONAL
DEVELOPMENT

There's a mental faculty that drives us into doing the things we do. The question I asked myself was where does this mental faculty gather its information? Why do we really do the things we do? The more books I read, seminars I watched, and digging deep into my own past I noticed there was an obvious connection with what I was reading, seeing, and hearing. All our lives, especially the first 21 years, we absorb ideas, morals, values, and life's general hacks from other people. We've listened to our families, teachers, friends, friends' parents, watched the shows they watched, listened to the radio channels they played, read the same newspapers they read and then once 21 rolls on by, we are tossed out into the world vending for ourselves. When something new, or something that we weren't quite expecting occurs to us, we resort back to all these little mental faculties that have been placed in our minds since birth. And if we can't find one, we find the closest thing and feed off of that. We then wonder why our life's falling apart, nothing seems to be going right, we're not in the job we dreamed of, family issues keep arising, and the bank flew by zero a long time ago. Well of course, we've never lived our lives. We've been living the lives of others, their ideas, their theories, their philosophy, and their outlook on life. This too might be a rude awakening, but sadly it's the truth that lays deep within our veins, streaming through our blood ready to breath air at any giving moment.

So what can we do about it? As with any problem, we recognize there is one. We can also simultaneously teach ourselves a new way of thinking. We do this by means of educational development. I don't mean to run out and get a degree right away. What I mean is we educate ourselves on a new way of thinking. As I sit and write this, I am reminded of my favorite part in a movie that many recent philosophers have studied, The Matrix. I've seen this movie a few times since its release and I never quite got it. Great movie, good action, but there is a message in it. I watched it again not too long ago and paused the movie on a certain part. I went back a couple of minutes and watched it again. It's the part where Neo was watching the kid bend the spoon. When asked how, the kid replied "there is no spoon". Wow, just wow, I finally got it. There is no spoon. I started to ponder this obsessively. As obstacles come my way as they do all of us, I am reminded that there is no spoon. How many spoons have we placed in our lives? What if we could all bend spoons? I'm telling you we can. We can bend all the spoons in the world and successful people know this.

We have to first empty our minds. I found this part easy as between my ears seemed empty to most... just ask my wife. We must dump the garbage. This part takes time since we have been stuck in our ways all our lives. The simplest way to do this is to be open-minded. Acknowledge what you think you know is wrong and start with a blank page (which we will discuss later). Start filling your mind with new ideas. Be a master of observation. Don't let anything come into your senses without your awareness, acknowledgment, and don't let it stay without your approval. I have split educational development into two categories that affect us all no matter what walk of life you come from.

Self-education: There truly is no other form of education than self-education. What I mean by self-education is being knowledgeable of every part of life you know you will encounter. Not once did I say be an expert, just be knowledgeable. For example, if you are about to lease a new house or apartment, it is understandable that you are excited and can't wait to sign. However, don't wait for a couple of months to pass when you receive a fine for something such as a friend's car parked overnight in the area without a pass. You didn't know you needed a pass because you just signed the contract without reading all the pages. When it comes to signing documents, many people will try and rush you through the process. Take them home for a night to read and research any questions you may have.

Ever been to a dinner party, friends or family's house, where everyone is talking and you feel really dumb and stupid because you have no idea what everyone is talking about? This is where a little research, and those person files come into play. You don't have to study hard. Just ask a few questions, read up a little on some potential conversation starters, then once in the talks, ask some questions. You'll find this helps with most people you know you're going to meet not just friends and family. You'll seem smarter, more approachable, and most certainly will not feel left out.

Ask yourself what you really want to know. Do you wish to know more about history, politics, science, or is it that you want to be more compassionate, loving, caring? Maybe you want to learn new skills, activities with family and friends. It's all out there. Books, seminars, groups, courses, classes, professionals, role-models, CD's, DVD's, YouTube videos, all the knowledge you want, for yourself to become the person you want to be is all out there. Not sure where to start? Try the library. It's free to join, it's somewhere to get away, and all the books are at your fingertips, all the knowledge in the world. No better place to start than somewhere that is free.

Work: Many people get up, get dressed, drive to work, and work a job they don't even like. Imagine telling the younger you... "you're going to grow up and work a job you hate just to pay the bills, and that's just life". Ridiculous absolute nonsense. You wouldn't dream of it, yet most people do this very thing. Want a promotion? New job? Then what are you doing about it? Moaning and complaining does nothing apart from creating a hostile working environment. I understand you have to do what you want to do in order to do what you want to do later. You should still use the process to learn. You have to be smarter than the next. You must become the go-to person. The person with all the answers. How? By studying. Study company policies and manuals and learn your job better than anyone else. Who cares if 'Jon' is naturally good at the job...become better. Go to classes, learn new skills, jump out ahead, and fight for every opportunity the company presents. You're going to get knocked down, and declined, and said No too. Educate yourself on how to deal with these 'spoons' and continue forward. A lion sees no other lion while prancing for its pray. Find out what the company's mission is and make it better. Find a mentor. If you can't find one, then have what I refer to as a virtual mentor...for me this began with Jim Rohn until I surrounded myself with smarter, more educated people. This challenges me and I am never short of mentorship. Put yourself in the job and position you want to be in. As your influences and self-education change, so may your ambitions. If you have a speech impediment and want to be a lawyer...do it. Remember, there is no spoon... Moses had a speech impediment and led millions on a long enduring journey. Let yourself work in the job you want.

THE HUMAN FACTOR

The perfect partner, the ideal dinner date, a polished physique, well-polished dress shoes, and a fat wallet are all images that we wish to portray. In the age of smart technology, we try more than ever to present ourselves in a perfect manner. Yet, today mental health cascades and suicides are at an all-time high. If only we could sit down and talk to ourselves in an honest manner. If only we could accept the negative and focus on the positive. If only we could become anyone we wanted to become. The hard truth is that you can. Later in this book we will discover the 'who am I' page. For now, we shall look at what I dubbed the human factor.

As a kid, I used to love watching TV shows such as Funniest home videos. Not because I enjoyed seeing others suffer. But because I could relate to the mishaps that we were watching. I took comfort knowing that I wasn't the only one who'd fall over after spinning a broom or falling off a swing. Growing up, I was influenced by the opinions of others. It was important to me that others saw me in a magnificent light. I had to make the perfect cup of coffee for guests, I had to have the nicest house, fastest car, fanciest clothes, yet all these tangible things cost money, the one thing I didn't have. All I learnt while trying to get others to see me in this magnificent fashion was how to get into debt.

Have you ever been in an elevator and someone farted? Quite possibly that was the most embarrassing moment that had ever happened to that individual. Why? Because everyone else automatically judges that person. But isn't this a normal function for the human body? Don't we all do it? So why would we judge someone else? Could it simply be that seeing others suffer from something that could easily happen to us makes us feel better?

We tend to look at positions instead of people. A great example of this are CEO's of big organizations. The second they make a mistake, it's plastered in every newspaper, news feed, and news broadcast available, and an up rise of instant revenge is demanded. I get it, most CEOs get paid a lot, and are expected to make the right choices, but this is unrealistic. No one can make one hundred percent right choices all the time. It's not possible, and they know this, but do you? Remember the person sitting at the top is human too. It's the same philosophy as a parent making all the right choices for their child. Every parent wants to, but I have never met a parent that has always got it right. We all need to stop looking at the position, and look at the individual instead.

Many people literally drive themselves crazy trying to impress other people. Albert Einstein once said if you judge a fish by its ability to climb a tree, it'll spend the rest of its life thinking it's dumb. Here's a thought for you… who gives a rat's ass? Why do you care about what others think? Do I think you should ever be satisfied with who you are? No. Because we should always strive for better. However, be the judge of yourself, not others. Never forget that a four star general, the president of the United States, Billionaires, and you all put trousers on the same way. There's no other way, it's the human factor. So next time you try

49

for that perfect date, laugh at the things that go wrong, such as food stuck in your teeth all night, or a spill of wine. Next time you want to show off your fat wallet, make sure your bills and deeds to your family are paid before you try showing off all the money you don't have. Next time you try posting that perfect selfie, ask yourself who really truly cares? I assure you no one apart from you, so why post it? We can never become who we want to be by trying to impress others. We all have faults, we all screw up now and then, and things don't always go your way. Accepting this truth will light the burden off your shoulders and begin the process of your self-transformation. So, the next time something goes wrong, someone laughs at you, or even worse, your tempted to laugh at someone else misfortune, just remind yourself its all apart of the human factor.

We all want to be the perfect mother, father, sister, brother, cousin, employee, and so on. We all wish that we hadn't told that one lie or that we were stronger willed to be able to help the un-abled and the disabled. In essence, it's the John Wayne image. It's the perfect image that we see on movie screens, magazines, online platforms, and influencers. What is failed to be discussed is how this perfect image is not only unrealistic, but also improbable to obtain. The amount of people who meet their celebrity idols, and then are immediately disappointed is unreal. That is because, just like you, me, and everyone else, we have what I call the human factor. This can be presented in many different ways and formats but I will try and keep this as simple and basic as possible. The human factor is knowing that your favorite superhero also has arguments with his or her spouse. The human factor is seeing a well-known millionaire conduct their own grocery shopping. The human factor is seeing a football player tumble the ball. The human factor is simply that all of us have to make a living, do certain tasks to attain our living standard, and finally the human factor is seeing that we ALL make mistakes.

I recall being in a meeting once, and the boss and his hedge-men were laying out plans for the future of the organization. It all seemed swell, and looked great on paper (I'm sure many of you know what I'm going on about here) yet in practicality, it just wouldn't work. When asked why, I replied "the human factor". The human factor has to make way for errors, even better yet, the human factor also has to make way for forward thinking and better ways to complete the task.

You see, humans are unique. We are the only species that can change the course of our direction in an instant. One thought followed by action has, can, and will continue to change the course of mankind, individually and as a whole, for the remaining of our time.

A major part of the human factor relies on three key things.

1. We have an undescribed, natural desire to always want and need to progress and grow
2. We have an enormous conscious that giving is the most important aspect of obtaining value
3. In order to progress we must learn from our mistakes. To effect change, we have to make mistakes in our un-explained desire to always move forward.

No matter how many times in life we cross our T's and dot our I's, we have to make way for the surprise of the human factor.

FUEL YOUR MIND

We have an understanding that we need to eat well to fuel our bodies, although many people neglect this and eat junk food consistently. We know that a vehicle will not move without gas in it, unless it's rolling down the hill and there's something to be said about that literally and theoretically. What many people fail to grasp is what is fueling their minds. The best way to discover what is fueling someone's mind is by listening to them. You'll soon discover that some people feed on drama, bad news, and gossip. Be quiet for a day and listen to the conversations that people invite you into. Listen to the complaining that surrounds the workplace. It'll be a hard find to find many positive people throughout the day. Too many people have their faces in their phones, concerning themselves with other people's lives rather than focusing on their own. We have this "fake happiness" for other people doing well, yet when we close our eyes at night, we feel incomplete and unaccomplished, riddled with envy for others who seem to be doing well. It was once said that we should stand guard at the gate of our minds, and how true. It took me a very long time to realize that even if my ideas, thoughts, and opinions are right, I can't change someone else's. I've argued and argued so many times trying to sway people into seeing my way, and it just wasn't happening. However, what was more important was that I didn't allow corrupt opinions and ideologies into my mind. I stood guard, deflecting all bad thoughts coming my way. For some strange reason people enjoy reading newspapers and waking up to the news, starting their days off with murders, road closures, and thefts. Even worse, many people look even further into it to see if it's someone they know, how bizarre. Pick up any book, listen to any podcast, or read about any successful individual. You'll find that they fueled their minds with books, ideas, and people who liked to think outside the box and believed that anything is possible. I heard a saying once that inspired me beyond belief, "nothing is impossible, just improbable". This means that against all odds, anything you and I want to achieve, we can. There is always a slight chance. Too many people will focus on the ten reasons why it can't be done, and all I ask we do is focus on the one reason it can and should be done. One reason that outweighs all the odds, all the disbelievers, and all the nay-sayers. Rest assured, all these people will grab onto your pockets once you prove them wrong, saying things like, "I always knew you could do it" and "I supported you the whole time". Forget these people, do what I do and hang around people that fuel your mind to become stronger, a believer, a better person than you woke up as, and most importantly, who believe in you no matter what.

If you want to become rich, read books written by the rich. You want a better marriage? Read books about successful marriages. You want a healthy body? Read books on health. It's all out there. All this stuff has been done before. All you must do is pick up the books, listen to the audio books, go to the seminars, and fuel your mind with inspiration. Only when you do this, you'll discover the thoughts that come out of your mouth will far exceed those around you. As with anything, with the right fuel, the right output will be achieved. What goes in must come out, it's law.

INSPIRE AND BE INSPIRED

One too many times I have seen people plead their case for why I should join them in their resentment or hatred towards someone. I'm embarrassed to say that I too have put forward a case in hope that others would join me in my misery and pitfall of dislike towards another human being. It took me many years to learn that hatred towards another person slowly kills the soul and drives a man to the brink of insanity. For many years I held hatred for one person. You see when I was a young teenager I was jumped and hospitalized by some other kids. I swore up and down that I would seek revenge, even if it meant jail. I now have a wonderful family that inspires me to be a better version of myself, and jail is just simply not an option. I learned that the act of forgiveness lifts weights that can only be lifted by a power unknown to humankind. Will I forget? No, that would be foolish. Forgetting is just as bad as placing your hand on a hot stove over and over again. I choose now to learn from my emotional and physical pain, and then I forgive those who I feel contributed to my hurt. I don't make friends with these people, nor do I trust them, however I do pray for the best for them, and leave the rest to God and Karma.

Another valuable lesson I have learned is that inspiration is the driving force behind any decision. I don't know what inspires you, or anyone else. I just know that inspiration comes from all forms of fashion. I find it amusing that one hundred people can listen to the same assembly yet get one hundred different opinions away from it. If you're not too sure about this, think of a political debate or broadcast and then listen to people's opinions on it. Nowadays you only have to open up social media to see that everyone has an opinion and they are mostly indifferent. Thus, the importance that I repeat, guide, and opinionate my ideas throughout this book so that you will be inspired to start making positive changes in your life. I do find motivation self-driven. I believe that only you can motivate yourself otherwise you're just asking someone else to do the task for you. Now when we need a little pick me up, the question shouldn't be 'what will motivate me?' the question we should ask ourselves is 'what inspires me?' Another food for thought here is why do we wait until we are feeling down to be inspired? Is it not easy to keep up when we are already up, so we need to ensure that our inspiration is being fed to ourselves daily, so that if we do fall, it's a mare trip rather than a fall.

I was watching one of those weight loss shows whilst at work one evening, and after three hours of this show I had had enough. If a 450 lbs. man can shred 315 lbs. in a year, I can surely get myself out of a rut and go from 220 lbs plus down to below 200 lbs., and physically be in shape. I was inspired by strangers on a television show. Ever since, I have taken one hour a day to myself to exercise. This isn't to boast, this is to demonstrate that even when I wasn't expecting to be inspired, a fire was lit beneath me, and I haven't looked back since.

What really gets under my skin is those people whom we meet in our journeys that when asked "how did you do that?" they twinkle their nose and claim it's a secret. No, no it is not. And I have made it my ambition to find out these so-called secrets. I have learned that once we accumulate knowledge, we tend to sit on it. Well that's like having food to eat, but never eating it. Eventually you die. So, we should start using the knowledge we acquire immediately. And, to make sure we have it right we should tell others about it. When someone asks me "how?" I sit them down and we discuss. The wealth of knowledge is to be shared, I assure you no one is going to steal your 'great ideas', they're available to us all, the difference is, some choose to use it, and some don't. I honestly believe that we should aim to inspire and listen to be inspired. If we all were to listen as if what is being said would change our lives, then it will. Now I know some people feed their heads with the wrong stuff. That's just part of the equation and the mystery of life. Why do some people choose to believe bad and hurtful things while others who have been hurt decide to dedicate their lives to helping others? We can't change them nor should we waste our time trying to do so. Be fruitful in thought that you are now changing your influx of inspiration and are willing to teach others. If someone asks, help. If someone asks you to do it for them, walk away. As Arnold Schwarzenegger said, "You can't climb the ladder of success with your hands in your pockets". Let others keep their hands in their pockets. Don't be ashamed that you are leaving them in the dust, no matter the guilt trip they may give you. You are your own person. Inspire and be inspired.

D.I.E

A word and thought that troubles even the strongest of souls. A fear that Napoleon Hill quite rightly labels one of man's six fears. It has been said many times over in many ways that we should face our fears head on. Therefore, I took this fear and learned to rearrange the thought process behind it.

You see, many people fall into the trap that we are on a timeline. That by the time we reach our thirty's, our bodies slow down, and by forty, we will either have everything we are going to have. We forget our dreams, our desires, our wants, and we fall into the sheep fashion and accept these as our realities and use them for our very own excuses.

Yet, as I was lucky enough to watch a Steve Harvey show, I was amazed that a sixty-year-old man decided to get into peak physical fitness. Another story I came across was the founder of KFC, the fast food chicken chain. Colonel Sanders was in his 60's when he established KFC.

It was my inner desire to go against the grain and change what I (and you as well) think about death.

It is possible, widely known and very much prayed against, that our lives can and will be taken from us at any given time. From the death of a new born child to a person a hundred years old. It's not often fair, and often very cruel. One may say that life is short, so we make use of what we got. Still most people put things off till tomorrow, and tomorrow, and tomorrow, and tomorrow just never arrives. The only death I greatly fear is the death of my dreams, desires, and goals to positively impact millions of people, and leave the world a better place than when I was brought into it.

I have come to learn that the fire of our desires slowly burns out. From the overweight individual that wishes to get slim to the woman who wanted to open her own company, yet got bogged down by family. The fire slowly dies.

Have you ever had all the passion and energy to do something then one day it just disappears? Maybe you listened to other people for too long and started to believe them that you can't do it? Maybe you kept using the sheep fashion as a daily excuse. Or perhaps you just plain simply brought into someone else's plan. Worst of all, you sold yourself-short trying to convince yourself this is as good as it gets.

The only death we should be afraid of is what I have coined 'Deteriorating Inner Energy', shortly put, D.I.E. You can feel her slip away from your fingers, the pip in your step slowly disappears, your appearance slowly decreases until you're wearing baggy t-shirts and pants all the time. This is death, the real death. This is the devil beating you at your own game. This is evil in its cruelest form. You may live to be a hundred but you may have DIE'd a long time ago. It is very possible, in fact most certainly, that most people walking the plains of the earth are already dead.

So, what are we supposed to do about it? The best under-standing I have of this is that we are to learn, grow, and obtain as much knowledge as possible. And don't wait to obtain all the knowledge to use it, else you'll end up like sheep. Learn, apply, learn again, and move forward. Yes, our bodies may slow metabolism down by our thirty's, but that's thirty years of knowledge we should have to overcome the weight gain, and to raise our mental and physical health to all new heights.

GOOD DIE YOUNG

As with many of us, the hurt of a child bothers me immensely. I use this bother as my why. I think of my own children and realize that life can be a cruel mistress. She can take life out of our hands at any given moment. This sickens me. My only comfort is that I may [and should] die before my children as that is the concession of life and that way it's supposed to be.

Needless to say, I do not have to tell you that we are all on track to our deaths. We all die, but some die young. It has been said that God has a plan for us all, and I truly believe that. I do not what-so-ever believe that we should leave fate in the hands of the untrusted. Some people walk around with their fingers crossed, hoping and praying that everything will work out. People generate bad habits by doing this, and with bad habits comes 'bad luck'. We have many things in our control, including the saving of money, the health and fitness of our bodies, the respect we give to each other, and the ability to love all and forgive the most hateful. Even if we apply all of these, teach our children young, and live by the morale code, the hard cold fact is that some people die young. Life is not always fair, yet with good habits we learn to weather the storm and regain dryness. I've known of many parents who lost their children at no fault of their own. They need not blame themselves, but more often than not, they do.

Why did I choose to add this little segment? Simple, it is a harsh and extreme reminder that life is truly precious, and at any given time, what we believe to be our reality can and will change in a split second.

"REACH FOR THE MOON, AND IF YOU MISS AT LEAST YOU'LLBE UPON THE STARS"...

LES BROWN

I heard once that there are only ten bad people in the world. You may run into them often, but there are only ten.

You can watch the news, listen to political debates, or even be silent for a day in your work place and just listen. You'll soon discover that the negative, the bad, and the pessimistic are usually the loudest, hence they are normally heard more. This may seem unfair, and that the majority suffer because of the minority, yet this seems to be happening all over the world. So what can we do about it? Simple, I learned that if I didn't like a rule, a judgment, or a direction of course, I would train myself, and work hard to get into a position to make a change. Toxic leadership seems to be a popular discussion nowadays, and I have my opinion on that. Weather I agree or not does not matter, what is important is that you, with dedication and termination can make sure that the right policies and practices are implemented. President Lincoln was known for making decisions that were right for the country, not what was popular. I draw inspiration from this and use it to guide me in making a decision. Many people won't make a decision for many different reasons, which are all underlined by one word...Fear.

Fear sees us huddled in the corner shaking with fright, making sure that others are out there gaining all they want from life; while we sit motionless, observing through the window of life, dreaming whilst drowning in our own thoughts.

God said plant the seed and I'll grow the tree. The trouble is many people don't even plant the seed. Now there's more to it than planting a seed. You can't plant a seed and not water it. You also can't plant the seed and then dig it back up. Needless to say, the seed has to be planted in good soil, where sunlight will hit it. But you have to plant the seeds.

More often or not, planting the seed comes in the form of decision making. This is what I've learned about making decisions. JUST MAKE ONE. If you're right, then good, and you'll reap the benefits of your choice. If you're wrong, then the human factor plays well, and you will learn from it, and move in the right direction. Either way, you can only win.

WHY IS IT?

Why is it that when things are going well, something always comes along and knocks you down? This is another question I pondered daily, and still do. I try not to think about this, however, when we are surrounded by lack, lack of moral grounds, lack of health, lack of love, lack of sense of well-being; when each week it seems some child who hasn't had the chance to shine the world with their ideas is tragically taken from the very earth that gave them life. It's hard not to think of lack.

At the end of the day I always draw the same conclusion.

If all our efforts are met with resistance and opposition, we ask ourselves why should we bother trying? And to that I say why not? Why not go out and give it a shot? Whatever ideas you're too afraid of taking action on, just go and do them. So someone told you no, it can't be done. AND? I truly don't understand where other people get off telling others no. Say yes to yourself, and start taking action. It will be the loneliest walk you've ever taken, however after every great journey arrives a beautiful destination.

From the moment we were born, a battle of oppositions occurred. When we first tried standing up, gravity knocked us right down. This didn't stop us from walking. We were born with the natural desire to progress. As we got older, we brought in other people's ideologies, and used them as our own excuses. Resistance and opposition are needed to help us grow and get stronger both physically and mentally. Bodybuilders tone their muscles through resistance training. It's not easy, nor do their muscles tone overnight. They work, show up and work again, day in and day out.

What are we supposed to do in a world full of negativity? Close our eyes and hope all the negativity will just disappear. This is borderline insane... yet this is what many people do.

Action. We must take action for anything to become a reality. Everything vibrates therefore, we must keep moving forward. If you're not moving forward, then you must be moving backwards...its law.

Think about what would happen to a brand-new house if no one ever lived in it. After a few years, the grass would be so tall you wouldn't be able to see the front door. There would be swirls of plants growing up all four sides. The pipes would rust and fall apart, and mold would infest the interior.

Now let's take the same house and move a family into it. The walls have a few dents in them, the kid's bedrooms have crayon marks all over the walls, the yard fence has a panel missing, and the kitchen faucet is dripping. YET, the house's value has gone up because the core of the house has been utilized which keeps all machinery in working order.

It is said that a ship that never sets sail rusts. And a ship that is battered by the sea works perfectly.

So, when you ask yourself, 'why is it? Don't forget to keep moving forward.

AH-HA MOMENT

As people spend their hard earned money to go listen to speakers, read stories of the rich and famous, or indulge themselves in an against-all-odds comeback story, they are guided to believe that there is an ah-ha moment. By all means there is certainly an individual choice made, yet that Hollywood ah-ha moment ceases to exist. I say this because as you read this book, I don't want you to think that there will be a moment where it all just clicks together and you jump up off your chair and charge on forward with all the might of the world. Instead I hope you will find thought-provoking ideas, theories, messages, and guidance throughout the pages. I hope you will be inspired to share a portion with a friend or co-worker. I hope you will find yourself pondering a portion throughout the day. I hope you will take action on something that stands out to you. Nonetheless, there will not be an Ah-ha moment. As we dive deep into the technological generation, our expectations of quick and easy answers and results have led many to believe that all we need is one Ah-ha moment. If all we needed was that one moment, then the people who won, inherited, or earned millions of dollars quickly would have managed to keep it all.

Instead, many lack inspiration, guidance, and knowledge, and we often read about how they managed to lose all their money. Let that not be you, as you prepare yourself for a future of riches and wealth that reach far beyond the value of momentary dollars.

KEEPING IT SIMPLE

L et's face facts and admit that we don't like to read between the lines. Men feel like women speak in code, and women most certainly don't need a million questions. It grinds me somewhat stupid when I'm asked a simple question and the person asking expects a detailed answer. Urgh! Anyway, it is my observation and experience that people don't like doing hard work. Being the bearer of bad news, hard work is something we can accomplish and will make us feel good about ourselves. What we do not want is the 'gossip' behind the mess. Meaning, give us the task at hand and we get it. Give us a run down on how you want every move to be made then do it yourself because no-one is listening. It's in that manner that this book is written, simple. I never said easy, and hard work must be followed, however it is very simple.

It is my belief that all the worries about that 'I'm pregnant' feeling have always been present. Where I must be humble is that whatever causes that feeling, I assure you is going to hold you accountable. All life's little issues you placed on the back burner have now surfaced. These issues are generally hacked down to five genera...

The relationship: The most important of all is the relationship you have with yourself. However, relationships with all whom we surround ourselves with are valued just as equally and can make or break you. We quickly become a product of our environment.

Health: You don't have to be a gym nut to live healthy. It is important to realize that all aspects of one's life cannot be filled to their fullest extent without a healthy mind, soul, and body.

Education: You don't have to go back to school. Education far exceeds the knowledge taught in a standard classroom. We should educate ourselves in all areas of our lives. Goals and dreams will become reality as long as we are educated in our chosen venture.

Work: Anyone can go from a line worker to CEO. Personnel development is key for attaining a great work ethic. Job knowledge is way more than just knowing your job. It's setting examples, creating opportunities, and reaching for the moon unlike any other.

Finances: The easiest of tasks which cause the most suffering, and to some, death.

We can assume correctly that each aspect naturally affects the other. Without one, the others won't work. It's a balancing act, and one you will struggle with. If we neglect one, we will most likely neglect the others. You can't start investing money when you have your family screaming for new household items. This can only happen when we communicate and create a plan. We can't get up to go jogging each and every morning without tasking our work aside and creating time. It is all vital, and such a complex system of trial and error. Give it time and the oak shall grow mighty. "A wise man can always be found alone. A weak man can always be found in a crowd." We all feel scared at times. A plowing train will come crashing off its tracks, and we must pick it up and put it back on. We MUST find the strength to do this.

Keeping life simple is dreamy. It always seems there is something in the way that strips us of our time. Whether it be work, family, friends, car issues, house issues, life just seems to hack us down to where most of us retire. At the end most people have nothing to show for it apart from the same pressuring issues that we've always had. I'm telling you it is time to simplify all these matters. Rami once said "Yesterday I was cleaver, so I wanted to change the world. Today I am wise, so I am changing myself". It truly does begin with a thought, a decision to make a change. It is just as easy to think big as it is small, so why not think big? Why not say screw it and think big? Why think of a hundred dollars to pay the bills when you can think of a million dollars to pay for your families' security? We waste so much time, space, and energy thinking and 'dreaming' small. I truly believe that one thought, one inspirational quote, one idea can change a person's life, and I hope this book is that for you.

JUST START

As my journey began, one thing became very apparent to me: I will never attain all the information I need. Think back to a time where you had to make a decisive decision. With certainty I can say that you didn't have all the information, yet you made a decision and rolled with it. I urge you not to wait until you think you have all the information. I ask that once you have a good idea, or have learned some good information, that you start applying it immediately. Everyone can talk a good game. We all know that one person that says stuff like "when my kids leave I'll begin my own business" or "After I see what happens with the stock exchange, I'll invest". These are all talkers and talkers never take action. Just start, take action, and keep showing up. You may not have the slightest clue in what you're doing and that's perfectly okay, as long as you're taking action. As I looked at all the struggles in my life, especially my period of depression, I always knew I had enough information to just start applying. The key was to keep showing up and keep applying what I knew. And I did. I kept showing up, day in, day out. I showed up more so on the days when I didn't even want to get out of bed. And to this day, I still show up and I still apply all the information I find valuable to me. Do the same and watch what happens. In a seemingly short period of time you will notice slight changes around you. When you're tired, hungry, sore, or sick, I'm telling you to keep showing up. You may discover that you're going the wrong way, and that's okay. At least you've discovered it rather than finding out in twenty years' time. This is the most important dynamic of personal growth. Show up and just start.

Every change in our lives begins with one idea, one inspiration, one action taken. I was never expecting my life to change, yet the simplest of ideas introduced to me made so much sense. I was no longer a fish out of water. Instead, my mind and body became lions of the jungle. Willing to run faster, be sharper, and become prime for the chaotic world we find ourselves in. We begin with the very first philosophy that turned my life around, and I hope yours too.

YANG

/ **Y**æNG; YäNG/▸n. *(in Chinese philosophy)*
The active male principle of the universe, characterized as male and creative and associated with heaven, heat, and light. Contrasted with Yin.

Through confusion we seek answers; the weak, strength; the poor, riches; the hopeless, hope; and the fearful, courage. While most find prayer in the hardest of times, we must learn to indulge in mindfulness in the moment. Understanding what is present, and how we use the moment builds a mental strength that even the Roman army would be proud of. To assist you with building up mental faculty, the following are some stories and ideas I have stumbled along the way that helped keep my interest keen, and my desire to search for more answers.

JUST AROUND THE CORNER

How many times are you going to keep telling yourself this? How many times will we allow others to convince us that whatever we are seeking is 'just around the corner'? How many corners are you going to turn? Only to find yourself in the exact same place. This makes no sense to the common man. If someone were to watch you turning all these corners...only to see you in the exact same spot, I'm sure they'd ask you why you keep turning corners. I'm sure that someone would eventually advise you that staying put and using what you already have in place may generate better results. Or maybe they'd guide you around an alternate corner... my question to you right now is this...how many corners are you going to continue to turn? And how come you never turned the right corner? The effort you put in COULD be the same, yet the direction is completely different. Many people mistakenly believe that success and achievement mean more sacrifice and effort. If you were to put gasoline in your windshield fluid tank, would the vehicle move? Or would the windshield be messed up by the gasoline? Now, if you place the same gasoline in the gas tank, we now have a moving, operational vehicle. Same gasoline, same vehicle, same effort.

All placed in the correct location. Be wary of the man who tries to sell you on the motion of his corner as your own.

WHAT A WASTE

Let's say a chef claims a meal took twenty minutes to cook. This meal is the best meal you've ever imagined. You think 'Twenty minutes, is that all it takes?' Well, NO. Preparation of the meal took over an hour. All the slicing, dicing, measuring, and heating the pans. It is here that the meal was created. Here lays a "secret". Ever wonder why it is said that you should think before you speak? The words that come out of your mouth will mean the difference of progression or digression. Imagine what would happen if a football team ran out on the field and just played without ever practicing? Could you drive a car without gas? We move so fast in our lives and yet most people don't even know where they are going. They're just moving, walking around ominously, talking on phones, speaking in meetings, without a single thought to what they're actually doing. Being in a rush will always slow you down. Just ask an Olympic runner. No runner would dare run that fast on their first day of practice. A breakdown of each millisecond enhances the chance of success. I don't believe that any one of us wakes up just to go to bed yet we fill the day with 'stuff'. A plan of the day will ensure that the 'stuff' is proactive. If only people took a minute to think, and seconds to speak. A moment of thought is like a turtle in your own very rabbit race. Thus is life.

We have a tendency to overcomplicate our lives. We add too much tension and resources where they are not needed. Our jobs have us anxious. If we don't answer our cell phones we will either be in trouble or have missed a big opportunity. Society nowadays has us all go go go. Emails and conferences right at our fingertips, it is too easy to get caught up in all the hustle and bustle. Ferris Buller famously said, "life moves pretty fast. If you don't stop and look around once in a while, you could miss it". It seems more so than ever that our daily endeavors last longer, seem more important, and time is seemingly not matching up with our days. I find that "too many people major in minor things" ... Jim Rohn. If we do not take time to reflect on our actions, then the go go go aspect of our day grabs hold of us and squeezes all the toothpaste out until there is no more. The tube is then thrown into the trash only to be replaced by a new one.

A SHOE BOX WORTH
MORE THAN A MILLION
DOLLARS

One evening a good friend and I were deep in conversation. He was telling me a story of how he kept a shoe box on his night stand. Now this friend was a lady's man at the time and entertained many women at his residence. Each woman who enters his home does so with one instruction: do not look inside the shoebox. No-one, I truly mean no-one looks inside the shoe box. Curiosity surrounded me as I yearned to know the contents of the box. I leaned in a little further and listened, ears pinned back, to his story. A lady friend who he had been dating for a while was lying on his bed fidgeting. Curiosity had riddled her and she went for the box. My friend was rightly upset and told her to leave. He stated "In the box is a thimble." The thimble itself holds little to no value. The sentimental value that it holds is priceless." His sister and he were very harsh on each other. Every day, even now as they approach their 30's, they push each other's limits in life; demanding greatness of one another. Now that I think of it, I don't really think I've heard a nice word said from one to the other, just demands and ridicules of "that's all you're doing now?" His sister had gone on vacation, and brought back a cheesy gift, said thimble. Cheesy to most, this was the first gift ever she had brought for him. He claims that to this day his sister will never understand the value of that thimble. To him, the thimble represents an undying bond of love and compassion. To him, the shoebox of memories is worth more than a million bucks.

AN APPLE

As I was listening to the twenty minute extract from the obtained success magazine, there was something that really jumped out at me. Mr. Rohn had made a statement and followed it up by asking his audience a question. He said "An apple a day... makes the doctor go away", in which he posed to the audience "what if that's true?" Now this got me thinking, what if that is true? And why doesn't everybody eat their apples, including myself? Mr. Rohn then went on to answer my question. He said "Just as easy as it is to do, it's easy not to do". And he was absolutely right. It was easy for me not to eat an apple a day for the past 30 plus years of my life. I'd been to the doctor at least six times a year, and was always feeling sick in some form or another. I wondered what else I had been leaving out. What other simple tasks have I been neglecting? I figured I'd put this theory to the test immediately, so off I went to the grocery store to buy a bag of apples. That night I ate an apple. The following day I also ate an apple. Every day I ate an apple and noticed slight little changes within me. I figured that if I was eating an apple a day, I better amp up my fitness game, so off to the gym I went, daily. I then figured if I was eating an apple a day, and heading to the gym each day, I might as well make better choices with my food consumption. I wasn't eating out as much, and noticed that the people I was being surrounded by had changed. I wasn't listening to drunk "I should of "story's at the bar of a restaurant, instead I was being influenced by successful people who had strict daily structures. By taking action on one inspirational philosophy, I started my ball rolling, and today the ball is rolling so fast it's a ride in itself to stay on board. As far as visiting the doctor goes, I go for my annual checkup and that's it. One thought, one action changed the course of my life forever.

WHO AM I?

A bond of character and love, a companion for life, and a ritual found in scripture. Without a doubt, relationships form the very fabric of ourselves, our family, community, and society. Relationships are formed from all the possibilities of life. You have the obvious dating and marriage, then family relationships such as brothers, sisters, mothers, fathers, some would even place friendships here, I most certainly do. Then we have the not so obvious ones such as co-worker relationships, the customer/consumer relationship and the social grace which I refer to as the bus stop relationship. Yet, the most important relationship that we are all in is one that very few talk about, many ignore, and even worse many do not realize its existence. That is our relationship with ourselves. I had a friend in England, who just recently passed away, who always told me "look after number one before you look after number two, number one being yourself". Ironically, the guy withered away due to his heavy drinking. After a year of reading all this 'personal development' stuff, I realized that everything that was going wrong in my life all had one thing in common...ME. To this day when something doesn't quite go right, a random argument with the missus, a creditor I failed to take care of, work troubles, and the little things that slip on us all, the first person I look at is myself. This may seem harsh to some, and at first it felt like a very unwelcome slap to the face. Yet, this holds true… Whatever is happening in your life right now is the result of the effort and choices you've put into your life previously. This is a straight up cold hard truth. At first you may want to throw up a natural defense… "I didn't ask for my dog to die, I didn't ask for my Mom to get ill"… I get it, and there are some things that we did not ask for, yet are inevitably going to happen. We know death is going to happen to us all, so if we know it's coming, what are we doing to prepare for it? Bad things happen to us all. I assure you that bad things are not just reserved for poor, unfortunate persons. Realizing I was the common factor in all 'bad' circumstances in my life, I wrote on the top of a blank page in my journal 'who am I?' Let me tell you that when I wrote that down I thought I was ready to go to town on the answer. Once I placed the question mark …nothing. Nothing came to mind. Everything I thought of was what other people thought of me, what other people saw me as, not what I believed was who I was. The 'who am I' page stayed blank for quite some time. I'd often flip back to it now and then just to see if I could spark some inspiration. After a couple of months, one day it occurred to me. At 35 years old I just clicked onto every purpose of each art class ever taken in school, every late night English essay, every science hypothesis. It never mattered about the context of all my efforts. What mattered was that each and everyone started off on a blank page. Each one started with the finish in mind. Each one was created from thought, placed on a blank page, and after hard work and effort, was complete. Whatever I wanted to write down, I could. And then make it work to be successful. So here I am, many years later, with a blank page pondering what to write. Whatever I choose to write, I can become. Not what others want me to be but what I want to become. This pivotal moment in my life means that I can take a blank page, write 'who am I' on it, and immediately start to become it. This is the best exercise I have ever discovered. I urge you to take some time and try it. Want to become a millionaire? Write down that you are a millionaire, and then become one. How? A penny at a time. Want to buy that new Xbox game? Instead, become a millionaire. Start writing and get extremely creative. Let your mind ponder and begin writing a new version of yourself. Imagine becoming more sophisticated. Write down 'I am a sophisticated person'. Study, learn (action) and become sophisticated. Don't wait, if you've learned a new skill mid-read of a book, don't wait to finish the book, implement the learned skills immediately. You'll already be changing before you finish the book... how exciting! How amazing. Truly think about this...with a blank page you can immediately begin to change your life. Best part...when you start to change and realize it is not who you want to be, rip up the page and start again. This is YOUR life, this is YOUR change. Don't be what others want you to be, be YOU. Don't know who you are? Then blank page away...start writing. I wanted to have a smarter, more sophisticated feel about me, so I wrote it down, went to a thrift store, brought some suits and dress pants and changed myself immediately. No one critisized me, in-fact they started to question me, ask me questions and wanted to know what I knew. All I did was buy some cheap pants. I started to read more, learn more, heed my advice to others, teach the lessons that I believed in so much, and here today I write this book for you, so you too can change and be whoever you want to be, and I hope you do this immediately, time is the only value we lose each and every second.

COMMUNICATION AND
SELF-PROJECTION

In businesses and homes across the world it is said that communication is the key to success, in both high-end businesses or happy families. That in mind, here we find the foundation of development. Communication isn't just the way we speak to others. Communication is how we walk, act, look, feel, and reflect. It is how we opinionate our thoughts and express our feelings. Communication is how we express ourselves in all forms of notion.

Nowadays it seems that nothing can take place without people all over the world hearing of it in minutes, sometimes even seconds. Technology has allowed us to connect with people hundreds and thousands of miles away within milliseconds. The 2020 Covid-19 pandemic demonstrated to the world how technological advances serve us. What used to be done by mail now resides in our hands. Zoom meetings, virtual family gatherings via Skype and Facebook Live. They all came to the rescue.

THINK BIG, AND IF IT'S NOT OUT THERE, THEN CREATE IT

I t's humorous to me how scared I used to be wondering what others thought of me. Nowadays, I personally keep my friends and family small and close to me. Other people, well, if they like me then I must be 100% on my game, and if they don't, they probably have no business sniffing around my endeavors. Perception plays a leading role when it comes to communication. If I am putting out the perception of confidence, I in turn will be surrounded by like-minded people. If I am being lazy and choose to walk the dog in my slippers, then perception is I am slob like. Perception is how we view others and how others view you. Why does it matter? It shouldn't, you're right. People shouldn't judge you for the way you look. Well, they do. Hard cold fact, they do. We can choose to communicate with confidence, even if we are not confident at all. Have a think about what you communicate on a daily basis. If you are unsure, ask, ask others what they think of your character. Watch people's reactions around you and see who you are attracting. Trust me, others will be real quick to tell you what they think of you. Here's a Dad joke I stumbled on, and I think it shows how one's perception can be viewed.

'A Roman soldier walks into a bar, holds up two fingers and asks for five beers'.

I cannot express the importance of communication. If I had to spend all my time teaching just one subject, it would be this. I recall a couple years back, the wife and I were arguing non-stop. I'm talking about arguing to where I was banging my head off a wall constantly. I was always saying "you don't understand me" and she would say "you don't listen to me". It would go back and forth all day, every day. I'd get to work and she'd be blowing up those text messages. I'd come home to constant nagging. It was brutal. What we did have in common were crime shows. We'd like to watch real life crime shows. As we watched these shows, I recalled when I was younger and was called to testify to an assault I had witnessed. After giving my account, thinking I had done great, the judge threw my testimony out. The judge had said it did not match other people's accounts. I knew what I saw, I didn't exaggerate, and told the whole account of what I had seen that night. Nonetheless as I was watching these shows many years later I concluded to myself that it is very possible, mostly inevitable, that two people seeing the same thing will recall two completely different accounts, and each one would be whole heartedly truthful. I was holding a coffee mug at work one day, and a peer commented that he liked the white mug I was holding and asked where I had brought it from. I told him, to which he replied, "I can only find ones that quote 'I love Texas' from there" (he was not from Texas). So I turned my mug around and in bold black writing 'I love Texas'. The point here isn't whether you love Texas or not. The point here is that we were both looking at the same object, at the same time, yet having two completely different experiences. I decided to present my side of an argument with a little communication. Before the next argument got heated, I said "my dear, please sit down and allow me to listen to what you have to say". Now I listened. I wasn't hearing the words to which I needed to counter argue for, nor was I holding an aggressive posture. I sat, listened, with one thing in mind…I created this moment, and I can change the future by changing me. I didn't need to be understood by my wife, I only needed to understand myself and opt to listen and listen well. I understand this does not always work, however most arguments stem from past grievances. We can't ignore them, so we must listen and deal with them. It may be uncomfortable, but this is where we find our true strength.

Question…Have family you wish to share the status of the pregnancy with and haven't spoken to them for a couple of years? Have you friends you think of often yet don't speak to? I'm asking you to change that. I'm asking you if you know you should have made that phone call, written that letter, sent that e-mail, to change that. Communicate your desire to pursue a positive relationship. A phone call does not have to be thirty minutes long. I call my mother each week, for a matter of ten minutes at a time. It's the THOUGHT that counts…remember that old saying…the THOUGHT, then think and do. Clean up that old mental mess of a to-do list. Have a loyal customer that you've been meaning to thank? Then take them to coffee, write a thank you card, and spend five minutes writing a personalized note to them. Before I continued to write this book today, I wrote a letter-style card to my eight-year-old son. He may not receive it for many years, yet my thoughts are with him and my love will be sent upon his readiness of understanding. Don't regret and ever wish you had. Do it now. Do the hard awkward work of communicating and mend those losses, bond those bridges, and strengthen the ties of the meaningful relationship of all people in your life as it is here where are mind wonders, as we think of what other may be doing, and the advice and comfort they may render as we build the strongest of relationships with each and all persons.

I have found that over the past few years, writing what I want to say to people has improved my communication a lot. I'm not talking about writing a speech, I'm talking about writing letters, emails, and thank you cards. Recall earlier I mentioned I wrote a card like letter to my son. I do this often. As much as I speak to him, I still write down my thoughts for him. I refer to them as my future thoughts of wisdom. And that's exactly what they are intended to be. As my son grows and develops, he will have these little deposits of wisdom, trust, love, all communicated through an act of thought and desire. Dead or alive, my communication with my son will continue to flourish, just like that of a singer who has untold amounts of unreleased material after their deaths.

Communication takes time which is an oxymoron since time is all we have. Yet it is the most important and valuable asset to any relationship. Just as an acorn sinks into the ground, years later it becomes the king of trees, as does communication. Make a deliberate and conscious effort to observe the way you address others. Do you tell someone you love them while folding your arms in a defensive posture? Are you excited during a family trip while not paying any attention to what is going on? Are you paying full attention to someone or something such as a presentation, a movie your kid wants you to watch, or maybe even a job interview, and your whole body is slouched in a chair? We must do better. We must be observant. Be a master of yourself and deliberately place yourself in certain positions. Watch what you are saying and how you look while you are saying it. Many great speakers of the past have all known this true fact; 70% percent of a speech is how you look, 20% is how you sound while delivering the speech, and only 10% is what you say. I don't know about you, but to me that tells a story. Sharpen up on those non-verbal's. Grab a book on presentations, non-verbal, and body language, read and PRACTICE. As the old saying goes, practice makes perfect.

Your way is obviously questionable, otherwise you would have stopped reading by now. I ask you to try my way. Make a deliberate and conscious thought and do it.

If your way hasn't worked up till now, then try mine.

If at this point you are saying to yourself BUT what if this happens? Or what if that happens? BUT if I do this, it may not work. BUT you've practiced this longer than I have. BUT I don't see other people doing it. BUT I don't have time to sit and practice. BUT BUT BUT. Here is the thing about BUT. I will keep it very simple. Once I heard what I am about to share, I started to notice the amount of times I heard, even worse, used the word BUT. I once heard, 'once the word BUT comes out of someone's mouth, stop listening, it's irrelevant. And I found this to be true. I found that everyone around me, including myself, was wasting time with the big BUT. I'd say to my wife, "Why don't we try this?" and she'd reply "BUT" … that's it, I stopped listening. Successful people don't need to hear the BUTS. They create answers, they find out how things work, and make them better. That's how success is achieved. Look at the car, one of the world's greatest inventions. Henry Ford took something that was already in existence and made the process better. And the whole process of building the car has continuously gotten better. Find out how things work, and make them better…starting with your communication. It was once said "Let's all be masters of our mouths, so that we won't be slaves of our words.

APPLYING KNOWLEDGE;
BEING THE EXAMPLE!!

My mother once said that you can always judge a man by his shoes. I'm not too sure how truthful that is, but I've always made sure to have clean, well-polished shoes my whole life. I re-call once being the youngest employee at a food factory (as I mentioned earlier). Somehow, they messed up my pay and promoted me only after a few months. My morals and values quickly set in and I went to speak to the boss, Dean. He said, "keep it, and prove to me you deserve it". Okay, I thought and quickly went off to prove myself. I got with the two old shop floor managers and quizzed them nonstop. I listened to their every word, made notes, and worked all hours of the day, sometimes 20 hours in one day. At the same time, we had a new floor overhead that acted as the liaison between the managers and the boss. No one liked him. The floor went silent upon his arrival. For some unknown reason he took a liking to me, maybe because he knew of my vulnerable proposition. He gave me more work than had to be done, and his methods were not suited for the work environment. Even so, something amusing happened. Eddy, one of the older managers, was prior military. I had some cadet training at that time and could relate to military jargon. Eddy started to shine his boots; I mean spit shine like he was back in basic training. I decided to follow suit. Truthfully, I knew I could get my boots shinier than Eddy's and enjoy a little friendly competition. This went on for a few weeks, and it became a running joke among us all. Meanwhile, our new overhead was confused, jealous, and upset because he did not know how to 'spit shine'. He'd bought the Kiwi buffer, and that was the extent of his shininess. During this time, I decided to wear nicer, smarter clothes to work. End of summer came, and the boss called me into the office and said I got the permanent promotion. Later that day Eddy and I were having a coffee, and he leaned over and whispered, "I knew those shiny boots would get you the job". And they did. They set me apart and made me lead by example. Later on, everyone on that floor had shiny boots, many got promoted and moved on, and as for the overhead, he got transferred to another factory. Eddy later died of cancer, yet I often wonder if he knew what he was doing by shining his boots. I'd like to think Eddy knew exactly what he was doing, he was sneaky like that.

The takeaway from this is that it takes one small change to lead the example for many. Eddy and Roger (the other elder manager) both willingly shared their knowledge. It irks me to no end when you ask someone a question such as 'how did you do that?' And they're like "no, no, that's my secret", like really? I'll find out eventually, and then surpass you, rest assured. They both were willing to teach their ways, and spend time so another person could perfect their skills. Twofold, I was also willing to learn, to become better, set myself apart, listen, and practice all my new skills. It takes both a teacher and a student for personal development to occur. Choose your teacher wisely. You wouldn't allow any old policeman in your house without seeing their credentials. Be sure you do this with your teacher and obtain all the knowledge possible.

One Friday afternoon nearing clock out time, throughout the time of proving myself to the boss, I was up and excited that the weekend was upon us. I intended to travel a couple of hours to pick up my girlfriend. We planned on going out, grabbing a few drinks, singing some karaoke and enjoying time with friends. Fridays were always fun and allowed us to release some tension and forget our issues, if only for a few hours. Turns out there were other plans in the making for me. One of the CEO's came onto the shop floor. They had an opening for a course due to someone being ill, and needed a person ASAP. I'm sure we all know that feeling. You know, the feeling of want versus right. Heck, I was about to get paid double time if I were to do this not to mention, I was in need of proving myself. So I did it. I upset my girlfriend, stood-up my friends, and decided to work into the night. The CEO made a comment to me that she could always relay on me (being reliable and being walked over are two completely different things, make sure you know which one you are in), and she could. You know those times you wish you had known earlier on in your life what you know now? Well, this whole story is about that for me. I never understood what was happening and why it all happened that way. I look back now with a full understanding of what happened. I can recall now that a few months later, after my hard-earned promotion, most of my friends were either in the same job, or had 'unforeseen' circumstances which saw them digress in their lives. On a whim, a couple of years later I left that job with nothing planned. I never knew why exactly I did that, but I do know I wasn't scared. I always had that internal feeling that everything was going to be okay.

What had changed so that I could keep that promotion? As well as my shiny boots, I had changed. I had obtained more knowledge relevant to a better job. I immediately applied my newfound skills. I became more valuable to the company. To this day, if a course is offered up I jump right on it and sign up. I no longer require those Friday nights. I have created a life I don't need to escape from.

In the book 'The seven habits of highly effective people' the author recalls a story that illustrates the simplest and most effective use of job knowledge. The story goes, A man ran a successful business. The business generated a few million dollars income each year. After a few years, the man died. Everyone assumed that after the funeral the wife, who inherited the business, would sell it as she had no idea of its industry. Few weeks after the death of her husband, she called a meeting with all the top heads. Assuming the worst, they all gathered around the conference table. She sat down. "Good morning" she said. "Good morning" came the mumbled reply. "What are we doing?" she asked. Looks of confusion glared through the room. "What are we doing?" She spoke. What works and what doesn't work?" she continued. As the answers started pouring in from all over the table, she sat back, listened, and said, "We are going to stop doing what doesn't work, and do more of what does work." This woman never did sell the business. She'd occasionally pop into meetings and ask those three questions. The business went from netting a few million to hundreds of millions within a short period. She was knowledgeable enough to know what to ask and smart enough to know she couldn't run the business on her own. She relied on those with the knowledge and led by example.

Take what you will from this, yet I leave you with a new take on an old but classic statement "the application of knowledge is power".

HEALTH AND EXERCISE

"Lack of activity destroys the good condition of every human being, while movement and methodical physical exercise save it and preserve it"...Plato.

There is only one square foot of real estate that matters, and that's the one between your ears. The brain being a muscle benefits from good health. Good health comes from diet, exercise, and fun. Now the ideas I share in this book are my own personal beliefs. There's an old native American saying "Now I don't know if it happened this way or not, however I know this story to be true". I ask that you read, do your own research and come up with your own conclusions. Health is important. I've kept this as simple as simple can be.

DIET

An apple a day. Yep, let me bring you into the know before we continue. I ate an apple a day, up until I read a new article that proclaimed the health benefits of eating two bananas a day over eating an apple a day. So I chose bananas, especially since I prefer them more so than apples. The point being I understand the health benefits of fruit. I also enjoy grilled chicken as a source of protein. What I don't believe is all these different diet programs. Each one of us in unique, and at this point in your life you should know what works for you and what doesn't. I feel a balanced diet is vital, but yet the strictness of it is self-dependent. I know people who eat what they want and stay thin and healthy all their lives, and others who eat greens and shakes yet can't seem to rid themselves of the weight. Proportion is key here. I eat the occasional fast food and know come the holidays I must step up my gym game. I snack on salsa and chips and don't deprive myself of my wants. THIS DOES NOT MEAN, nor is it meant to give you a free ticket to eat whatever you want when you want. It's just simply saying that there is a balance within you, and it must be found. See a nutritionist, read health magazines, maybe even find a scheduled diet that works for you which is the point I'm trying to drive home here. It must work for you. Stay away from sodas (seriously, have you seen what a soda can do to a coin....yuck). I drink a lot of water. Logic and reasoning tell me that if our bodies are mostly water, we should replenish it. I truly keep things simple. I also know the feeling after eating junk food. The feeling of tiredness and laziness. I know that food is fuel for the body. You wouldn't put diesel in an unleaded car, not just once, ever. Keep that in mind as your body is your vehicle. You need it every day. Research online, ask some friends, speak to a professional, and find a good diet that works for you that keeps the body energized.

Books!! Many times I have mentioned, and will continue to mention the importance of books. And, the importance of writing things down, such as keeping journals. What does this have to do with diet? As mentioned, the brain is a muscle, and needs refueling too. All the knowledge in the world can be found in books. We call this "food for thought". Just as with food, be mindful of what you read. If it's junk, keep it very minimal. Body and mind are often linked together. Keep them sharp and fuel wisely.

EXERCISE

" *All parts of the body which have a function, if used in moderation and exercised in labors in which each is accustomed, become thereby healthy, well developed and age more slowly, however if unused they become liable to disease, defective in growth and age quickly"...Hippocrates.*

Find someone who has never done a push-up before and ask them to do one. Watch a child who has never walked before sail across the room flawlessly. It will not happen. As parents hold a new born, they steady its head until the muscles are strong enough in their neck to hold their own head up. We all must train each body part and keep the skills homed therefore we do not lose their use. I find the trouble here is that we cannot physically see a lot of our body, in-turn we neglect it. Lungs must be strengthened by cardio, yet many people smoke and weaken them. What you don't use, you lose. Look around and you'll find this to be true. You wouldn't ask a child to skip the crawling phase. So, what happens as we grow older? We get complacent. We buy into other people's philosophies. We see elders that smoke, not truly seeing the internal damage, yet we buy into the visual of habits. We become lazy. Xbox, PlayStation, Televisions, cellphones, drive-thru ATM's and fast food have made us lazy. I'm not saying don't indulge now and then, I'm just answering the hardest of questions in the simplest form. With all that being said, it is my take that the body should be exercised daily. This doesn't mean pumping iron at the gym every day. It means move, be active, create a household environment of moving around. If you know for the betterment of your health you should take a walk, even if it's just to the mail box, why is it that some people don't? Just as easy as it is, it's just as easy not to do. The best part about exercise isn't the actual exercise, it is at the end when all is said and done and you can say "wow, I just did that". Find something that involves others. Bike riding, swimming, soccer, throwing a football. Whatever it is, find something. In summer I would come home from work and throw the ball with my son. I kept track of my steps with my watch (highly recommended). I made mention to my son of my step count goal, and we'd double it while having fun. Create the type of environment that works for you. I personally get up early, run, lift weights and in the evening play soccer. I do this alone as I use this time to think. I do this early for two reasons. I'm alone and it is quiet, and in the simple mind set I have, I wake up and start the day on zero calories. Working out in the morning sees me start the day at around -1500 calories. I could eat 2000 calories and still burn fat. Fantastic and simple at its best. That's just how I think though. Once again, I urge you to find an exercise plan that works for you and make it fun.

HAVE FUN

I recall as my mother was cooking food in the kitchen, I would grab and stand on a chair and start dicing cheese. I'd wash some lettuce and chop some tomatoes and make a basic salad. To this day I enjoy a healthy salad. Why? Partly because I wasn't allowed to cook at such a young age. I thought I was doing fantastic making dinner for the whole family. It was fun, and valuable time I enjoyed spending with my mother. My wife, son, and I walk the dog in the evenings. We discuss the day's events and enjoy the evening sunset. My son and I decorate the house. Whatever works for you, tie it into your day and make fun of all you do. I used to dislike running; I now know that it is the only time people truly leave me alone. I make the most of it all. If I am frustrated, I will go and lift some weights while listening to music. It releases inner tension. That's what works for me. When my son was in the crawling stage, I used to do push-ups on the floor. He would try and mimic me by bobbing his head up and down. Not only was this hilarious, but I also realized that I was teaching him good habits. Start now, don't wait. Do something. Something is better than nothing. Eat an apple, change your routine, do a few pushups, walk to the mail box, walk the dog, and let it all settle in as you become more knowledgeable and educated. Start now and watch your whole day turn around.

WHEN YOU HAVE A MILLION-DOLLAR VISION, DON'T SURROND YOURSELF WITH ONE-CENT MINDS

There are many valuable lessons to be learned in this book. If you have come straight to this section and money is all you care about, I assure you, you will not be successful. You can't win NASCAR just because you have the fastest car. You must be smarter than that. For those who have read patiently, I thank you. I hope you've taken many good notes and have become a new student of desire and life. Handling money is truly simple. Yet, becoming an unshakeable character speaks more than fiscal wealth.

When it comes to money most of us have been caught up with these buy now pay later deals. We apply for store credit to save 20%. We are roped in by low to no credit...no problem we finance here. As much as I enjoy the benefits of a credit card, I too was once stuck with thousands of dollars in debt. It's common, and, furthermore, it's almost expected nowadays. I once overheard a conversation in which the guy claimed, 'Yeah, I'll be out of debt next month, minus my car and house, that's always going to be around'. That struck a nerve with me and irritates me every time I think of it. Why? Why does this always have to be the case?

Since striking up conversations with random people and asking, 'will your car and house debt always be around, and if so why?' I am amazed just how most people actually agree with the testament of that one man. Sadly, I believe it is because people feel 'that's just how life is'. My old neighbor across the street and I were having a discussion about finances. I told him my plan of paying off my mortgage and being debt free. He exclaimed, 'It's too late for me to do that'. Let me tell YOU right now; I don't care if you're a child, in your teens, twenty's, thirty's, forty's, heck even in your seventies, IT IS NEVER TO LATE TO CHANGE, PERIOD. If you choose to advise others remember not everyone you advise will be listening. They heard you but they didn't listen. Don't waste time letting butterflies free whilst you're in a bird cage. At least set the butterflies free outdoors where they have a chance to fend for themselves. Some will be eaten by birds and that's okay. Let us ensure that not all birds have full stomachs.

I could talk about finances all day. The entrepreneur in me always ventures for new ideas while simultaneously sharing wealth with those in need. I read many books involving income and finances, and am continuously updating my financial plan. To keep it simple, I have narrowed finances into three parts. Bills, savings, and investment. There is much more to finance than this, yet if you adjust just those three you'd be set for life.

It is important to have a financial goal. Not just a goal of a million dollars because it sounds good. A goal that has a purpose and will challenge your every being. When I first started my personal journey, my goal was financial independence. That means that I owe no one nothing and I could live off the wealth of my own assets. I started off small by getting rid of my cellphone company and going to a no-plan company. Not only did this save me $100 bucks a month, I owed no-one nothing in regard to cellphone bills. I then looked at a big-money-ticket item, my car. It occurred to me that buying a brand-new car was one of the worst financial things I've ever done. Selling my car, and buying a car in cash, in my personal opinion, is the best option. I can buy a car that suits all my needs, spend half the cost, and any upgrades I wish to add on such as a new stereo I can do that and owe no-one anything. Yes, you'll have to save and yes you may have to sacrifice a few miles; however, I can't explain the feeling of owing no-one nothing. The biggest ticket item on my list is our house. When the wife and I were renting I discovered cars don't make profit, houses do. So, we bought a house, put a thirty-year mortgage on it and decided we'd have it paid off in ten years. Therefore, after ten years, we have a financial structure to aid in our future.

CHILDREN'S COLLAGE

W e then discussed our children's university education. If we are to offer to finance our children's university education, they should earn it. When my children enroll in university, my wife and I will cover the expenses for the first year. By the end of that initial year, they should have earned enough money to pay for the second year. We will then cover their expenses for the second year. This pattern will continue until they graduate. What will they do with the money they earned? Continue reading and you will soon discover. It will quickly become evident that graduating from university without any debts and with a substantial amount of money is achievable... all it requires is discipline, hard work, and the determination to succeed. It's only four years of persevering; just imagine the possibilities that await after developing such a strong character.

BILLS

Making minimal payments on bills gets us nowhere. I wanted to be financially independent therefore I wondered is it possible to become rich, while paying down bills? The answer is yes, absolutely. To me there's no other way to do it. If you are in debt and acquire the knowledge to learn how to be financially independent, then you must act immediately. If you are in a maze and not sure where to start, the book that helped me out and served as a step-by-step guide to getting rich while eradicating debt was David Bach's The Finish Rich Workbook. Step by step, you'll learn about your own self-worth, your true value, key items to take care of such as wills and insurance, and how to manage that debt while aiming for financial independence. This book opened my eyes and served as my own personal advisor until I could obtain an advisor of my own.

SAVE

If you remember earlier in this book I spoke of a book that I was so excited about, I rushed it out to all my friends. That book was the beginning of my financial independence. George S. Clason's The Richest Man in Babylon. That book brought to light the basics of handling money. There's a concept that goes with handling riches, and this book lays it out in the simplest form. One key point to riches, as pointed out by near enough all millionaires and financial advisors is to save at least ten percent of all your income. To some this may sound like a lot, and to others maybe saving more than ten percent is easier. What you will notice is that once you get into the habit of saving, you won't even notice the money is gone. Point proven, ten years ago I was court ordered to pay child support. I wasn't making a lot of money at the time, and near enough was living pay check to pay check. $735 was the ordered amount to pay every month. I was also required to provide health insurance for my son. $735 was defiantly more than ten percent of my income. You know what I learned? I learned to adjust and after a few months I didn't even notice it was gone. I learned the basic principles of obligation and discipline. It felt good knowing I could achieve such a basic financial task and be okay. I was okay, I had survived. I had a roof over my head, three meals a day, a cell phone, friends, and family. Heck, I had cable TV too. The fact is I was scared, confused, angry, and didn't know how I was going to afford my responsibility. I held onto faith. Faith that everything was going to be okay. I trusted myself to make hard choices. I went without some luxury, and still lived better than a lot of people. I was grateful for what I had and humbled that I had the means to pay my dues. If I can do it, I hold faith and trust that you too can today make the choice and start saving at least ten percent of your income.

INVEST

I nvesting is risky, so what? Give your excuses to the birds. We invest in our bodies with good diet and exercise. We invest in our work place by attaining valuable knowledge and skills. We invest in our relationships through commitment and common goals. We invest in ourselves with personal development. So why not invest in our financial future? It's all risky, and yet the benefits far outweigh the cries of disconcert. Mind that portion where I advise you to educate yourself on everything…this is one of them. Know enough so you are comfortable with your investments and be aware that you are not the financial advisor. We go to personal trainers for fitness, a cook for good food, a nutritionist for good diet, the doctor for good health, and a pilot for a safe flight. Who on Earth ever told us to trust ourselves with money? Seriously, most of us are not experts. Most banks have free financial advisors. All you need to do is set up an appointment. My financial advisor set up a one-hour telephone meeting with me for our first introduction. He asked me about my family life and made me feel very at home. As we talked he was viewing my minimal bank account. When he asked me about my financial goals I said want to be a millionaire. He didn't laugh or mock me, nothing. He went right into how with an action plan. He set small goals along the way to ease the burden of the big goal. These small goals help me daily and each time I reach one, I celebrate. A steak dinner, a few laughs with friends, it doesn't matter, I just celebrate. My friends are unaware of why I celebrate as I see no need to gloat. Gloating is for show-offs and in my experience, show-offs usually end up broke, hurt, and lonely. Humility should be present in your well-rounded character. Investing helps reach financial goals, and let's face it, if your all eyes and ears reading this, then trying a new way won't hurt.

Before we continue let me attest to something. There is a major difference between financial plans and financial budgets. A plan is what we will discuss here. A budget is where you pay your bills and live off of. We should all have a plan. A plan is a goal with perimeters. It sets the tone of how you wish to proceed. A financial plan doesn't have to be complex, just strong and exciting. I will share with you one of the best financial plans I have ever come across. It is so simple and yet makes so much sense.

70% budget. Pay bills, buy groceries, get gas, whatever it may be, just live off 70%.

10% savings. Saving money satisfies our inner need for security. It allows 'rainy days' to happen. After a while when it hasn't been raining, you can take your savings and pay off some debt or treat yourself to a vacation. If you use your savings it's important to start saving all over again.

10% Invest. At an average of 10.2% percent (based on the average S&P 500 over the last fifty years) this is how 10% would look if $468 was invested each month:

Year(s)	Savings
1	$5,158
5	$31,615
10	$82,996
15	$166,501
20	$302,214
30	$881,230
40	$2,410,579

To be real to be true, do the math yourself. Now, if you double your income, this is what it will look like:

Year(s)	Savings
1	$10,316
5	$63,230
10	$165,993
15	$333,002
20	$604,427
30	$1,762,459
40	$4,821,157

Can you imagine teaching your kids this? At age 40 they can choose to retire. I see no reason why anyone wouldn't want to put this into practice. This is basic investment at its best. The riskier you are with investments the more return you could potentially gain. There is always a chance you could lose it all, however 10% savings should be doing the exact same thing, therefore you are on track to your riches.

Another point I'd like to drive home is that if you lose your investments due to market crashes, bad investments, or whatever the case, it's only 10% of your money. It doesn't matter if you lose ten dollars or a few hundred thousand; it's only 10 percent. Having an optimistic mindset will help you stay the course no matter the outcome.

DONATING

I contemplated whether or not to write this into the book. The reason being is that there are people that only want to self-serve. Then I realized that you wouldn't be reading this book if your intentions were purely selfish. We should teach our children at a young age to cough up 10% of their pocket money. Teach gratitude young so as they get older the habits are already settled in. One of the world's wonders is that gratitude reciprocates. I'm not exactly sure why that is. I like to believe that rendering service is our responsibility, and a service well rendered will be paid to its deserving. Good things do happen to good people, more so to those who want nothing in return of their gestures. We can see people all the time doing wonderful acts of kindness and donation, only later to moan about how it hasn't paid them back. Selfishness is good grace that has been infected with the disease of evil. This type of people may see the return they are after. And I ask at what cost? Did it cost them a friend? A family member? Their home? Or maybe it was the cost of loss in faith from another. We are absorbed in a generation where people feel the need to know how everything works. Where faith seems to have been replaced by justifications and excuses. I have been asked many times how donations are reciprocated. I pondered this for a few years and came up with a hypothetical. Here I will lay out an example of how generosity works. Let it be known that this example may seem harsh and selfish. Neither are my intentions. My intention is to simply show how giving comes back around tenfold.

A man lost his job and is feeling pretty low. He goes home to seek comfort from the wife. Five steps in the door, he looks at his wife's drooping face as he fears to bear the news to her. She claims they must speak, and so they sit down and talk. She tells the man she is leaving him, filing for divorce, and she is selling the house. Upset, the man now goes to the bar to drink his sorrows away. He learns that his friend who was supposed to be at the bar an hour ago just died in a car wreck. If disaster struck all at once, this guy certainly felt pain. Suicidal, depressed, no home, job, wife, and loss of a friend. Another gentleman noticed him. He offers a prayer and takes the man to a Sunday gathering at a local church. Now this man is not religious, but something the minister says that Sunday sticks with him. Only he knows what resonates with him. But one simple quotation stuck in his mind. He started to look at things a little differently. Applies for many jobs, eventually getting a well-paying job. He gets himself an apartment, nothing fancy, however it's his. He starts hitting the gym, bettering his health. He visits his lost friend's grave site looking to close that chapter of his life. He decides to go out one evening. This evening he meets a woman. They connect and end up dating. The man's life has turned around and he is nothing but optimistic ever since that day at church.

Already we have many examples within this story of compassion and giving, however there's more. There is more than just that kind gentleman offering a prayer, the minister saying some words of wisdom, the gym staff who helped him along his fitness journey, the apartment complex that worked with his situation to meet his needs, and more than the woman who saw something in him to give him a chance. So, what's missing? Here's the part of the story that's missing. You, yes YOU, donate a small portion of your income to that church that the man happened to go to that one Sunday. Because of that church's good graces, the man's life started to turn around.

Now back on his feet, the man goes shopping every week for groceries. Every week he buys a product that YOU and YOUR company make and puts on the shelves. Because you donate to a church, which keeps that church operational. Because a kind gentleman was inspired and kind enough to help a man deeply troubled. A once troubled man now making a good income chooses a product that you've designed, engineered and produced which in turn pays you ten-fold.

Please understand all this is hypothetical. I believe that this story illustrates much more than how generosity pays back. If someone decides to give for their selfish benefit, I hope the sacrifice of an ill mind and darkened heart carries heavy upon their soul of dishonesty.

This portion of the book may seem smaller than you expected. Some of you may of wanted a step-by-step guide. This will defeat the purpose of personal self-growth. You have to want to help yourself and be willing to do the work. I've discovered that money comes after you're disciplined.

WHEN ARGUMENTS
HAPPEN

Most councilors, speakers, and self-proclaimed help books tend to ignore or just brush over this topic. Many speakers will portray a "happy" lifestyle with the perfect relationship. I think both you and I are smart enough to know that relationships don't work that way. As mentioned many times throughout this book, we have to be prepared for the worst. Even in our relationships. To explain my point further let me tell you a story of what recently happened between the wife and I. We live in two different states due to the nature of our work and some nights are harder than others. I miss my family dearly and I know she misses me. She looks after our daughter, is full time employed, and is taking her last two classes for her degree. Remarkable as all that is, there was a recent night when my mind was overthinking. I was getting pressure from work; I was a little overwhelmed and needless to say my mental health was not great on this particular night. I went off the deep end and started a full-blown argument with my wife. I said some things I regret (remember, words are powerful) and it became a big ordeal. My wife then did what I think was the most honest and respectful thing she could of done. She gave me tough love and straight up ignored me. At the time I felt as if she shunned me but what she was doing was divertingly holding me accountable for my own actions. Sometimes, walking away from the situation is better than arguing about it. I wanted the argument, I wanted to fight through our issues, and she walked away. I felt horrible. I questioned her true love for me, and how someone could just ignore their husband/wife. Now I look back at it and realize that arguments happen and when they do it's sometimes best to walk away. I replayed that argument in my head. Convinced I was right at that time, and knowing she was too, I mentally forgave her. Forgiveness doesn't have to be an all-out apologetic state or forgetting what happened. Forgiveness can be leaving it at the door and moving on. I love her dearly. Now and then she pisses me off and that's okay. I know for the fact that I piss her off daily, she'd probably argue hourly. An argument doesn't mean running for a divorce or using that argument to have a drink. Arguments are going to happen and some arguments need to happen. Doesn't change how you feel about the other person. Sometimes it's beneficial to argue through the difficulties, however, let's not actually fight one another. What I want you to get from this is not to prepare for an argument but to understand that arguments happen. And it's not the argument that matters, it's how you deal with it.

PART NEGATIVE

As we scroll our phones, read our books, and listen to sermons, the message always seems to be 'stay positive'. Don't get me wrong, a positive attitude will always get us further than a negative one yet once reality sets in, life's a bitch. I deliberately use yin and yang in this book to remind us that life is part negative. So how do we deal with this? Whether you have a job or not, you're not in the job of your choice, or want to work for yourself...whatever the dream and goal is, you must understand that there are no straight lines in nature. You will experience pain in the meanest of fashions. We must acknowledge that no system is ever completely perfect. If you're not employed, then get employed. Not that easy, I don't care! I truly don't. Life should not be easy. We can't have hot without cold, yes without no or, win without losing. You certainly cannot have a job without trying. The law of averages will see that you will succeed upon a lengthy medium of attempts.

It rains on us all. I always say the difference between the rich and the poor is that the rich do two things; check the weather and carry an umbrella. We must learn to weather the storm. Most people are trying to stop the storm...that's plain old stupid. If you are applying to be a manager and haven't even earned your GED, then you have to re-evaluate. It's possible for that manager position to be yours with the right education. We hear consistently of politicians fighting to raise the minimum wage. Why does it matter? Why does in matter what the minimum wage is? Unless you're planning on staying at the bottom, the minimum wage doesn't matter. I'm yet to meet a successful person who's lived off of minimum wage. It bears truth that it's quicker to climb the ladder of success than to fight and stay at the bottom. Put those mental boxing gloves on and fight your way around that thought. We need not worry about how others are doing, and how they are doing it. We must worry only of ourselves, therefore, ensuring our future, our family's future, and our children's future are filled with work ethics and morale compasses that would make the pope blush.

LEAVE IT BEHIND

The rear-view mirror in the car is small for a reason. We don't drive down the road staring into the rearview mirror. We drive, looking at the road through a nice big windshield. Occasionally, we glance to see what is behind us. So why is it that so many people drive their lives staring into the rearview mirror? No wonder so many people hit roadblocks. It is vital that the rearview mirror of life be present, and we should glance, reminding ourselves of what is behind us. As we do this, we may realize we missed our turn...the best thing is the big old windshield in front of you will allow you to turn around and re-attempt. If you find yourself staring into the rearview mirror, turn your head slightly and look at the whole scene.

As we glance back we find we all have some things that make us feel sick, disappointed, upset, or angry. For some this may be the gaining of weight, others a missed job opportunity or having a failed relationship. No matter the past, we add those experiences to the leather of our souls. Our history does not and should not define us. If we were to take all the hard-earned lessons and apply them to one year, we'd have the best year ever. We will soon discover that we know what not to do as well as what to do.

And as long as we keep applying what we've learned, our lives will continue to get better and better and better. It was once said that "when we run towards our goals, we automatically leave our past behind us". Let us not walk into the past. We must not walk forward with our heads turned backwards. We should only use our past as a direct way forward.

MILITARY VETERAN
LESSON

M any, if not most of us have a military veteran in our family, or at least know one. As a young teen I used to love going to the bar, sitting down with the older veterans and being indulged in their stories. Some were funny, many were gruesome, and others were just plain eye openers. All, however, were personal. What I noticed was a pattern within these stories which featured three foundational traits that were re-occurring and seemed to be vital to the success of the outcome. A few years later I found myself living by these three basic principles. I'm aware that they are fantastic military strategies, yet upon inheriting them on a personal level, I saw myself fearless. I share these lessons with you hoping that you decide to take them on. Truly think about them, and adopt them into your everyday endeavors.

1. There is no such thing as a dead end. If you can't go under it, over it, or around it, you must go through it.
2. Always advance towards your enemy. There is always someone or something ready to attack what you have and take it away. Advance towards the enemy and

protect what is yours. If this was not important, sport teams wouldn't have an offense.

3. Never lose ground that you've gained. There will be times where you have to retreat and that's perfectly fine. Regroup and attack. Flanking works well here. In turn you regain the ground you had, and if flanked correctly, more ground than you started with.

I find the personal depth of these three traits helps me tackle any, if not all, resistance and obstacles that are in my way. They harness a mental toughness that without them, the world would pray on the shallowness of lack and limit. What dead ends are you facing right now? Which way are you going to choose to attack those obstacles? Is it over, under, or around? What enemies are lurking in the shadows of your very own thoughts, hard work, and family? What enemies are trying to attack you and take away what you've gained and earned? Maybe it's your very own thoughts? How are you going to advance towards your enemy? Is the enemy already attacking? What best way are you going to flank? Can you see more potential behind the advancing enemy? Reach. Reach as far as possible and gain more ground. You're already at war, might as well make it worth it.

GROWTH

I f I were to stop writing, it would be here. This is where the end of all rests. It is here that we become what we choose. It is here that we develop our skills, our knowledge, our bodies, our strengths. We rid ourselves of our weaknesses and create empires of our minds. I cannot express the importance of continuous growth. It was once said that "if we aren't moving forward, we must be moving back"... again, It's law". Now I'm a law-binding citizen, and let me tell you, if someone convinces me it's law, I obey. I realize I'm not going to get arrested for not developing myself, however I fear I may end up worse. Homeless, stupid, broke, sick, with a family that doesn't want me. Don't believe me? Think of the amount of homeless veterans living in America today. Each one had a family. I would say they had two families, personal and military. Families promised to never leave another behind and now they live on the streets with little to show for the hard sacrifices. So we should ask what happened? Drugs, depression, PTSD, and other like issues yet I believe there is another reason. People just don't develop themselves any further. There is help available for any situation, ANY. The human mind naturally wants to develop. When someone runs, they want to run faster. A pitcher wants to throw better, a salesman wants more sales, and artists desire creation. For many, parting with time becomes the excuse. I admit it is hard to wrap one's head around the dilemma of parting time for something that may not even be beneficial. I truly understand that when we work, come home, eat dinner, spend time with the family, the next thing we know it's past our bedtime. I get it, I truly do. This is where faith prevails. We must part time before time parts us. Trust that progression far exceeds regression. Starbucks is a fantastic believer and example with this. Starbucks continually improves its chain, developing their products and their employees. Starbucks CEO stated that "just because we made a lot of money, doesn't mean our mission is done. We must continue to improve". American football quarterback Tom Brady is the pinnacle of all this. Tom Brady is in the record books with the greatest comeback of all Super Bowls, Super Bowl XLVIII. 39 years old (which is ancient by NFL standards). Tom Brady dismissed conventional wisdom by playing extremely well for so long. Upon his return to the NBA, Michael Jordan was told he would never win another trophy and that he was too old. Instead, realizing his older age, he changed his workout routine, fueled his body with the right nutrition, and led the Chicago Bulls to three additional championships in 1996, 97 and 98. The common factor is continuous growth. They knew what had to be done, educated themselves, dedicated the time and energy and reaped the benefits.

Be smart. If you want to coach a soccer team, you must research soccer tactics. You'll find that many others have done this before and written about it. Learn from other people's mistakes. Take the short cut, it's okay. You'll save much time. It's plain old stupid if we watch someone burn their hand on the stove, then we follow suit. We witnessed the pain, saw the scares, so why repeat? It always blows my mind when someone smells something of dislike and then asks you to smell it…ummmm, NO, not going to happen. I watched their reactions and quickly educated myself that indeed it does smell disgusting and I do not need to smell it. We must use our minds for education and our brains for decision making. Find out what the unsuccessful are doing, and don't do it. It truly is simple. Remember, the wheel doesn't have to be reinvented, just improved. The wheel made many people rich and drove the opening of many businesses and all that was done was improvement of the wheel.

CHANGING THOUGHT

Just because people love us and are willing to die for us does not mean they know what is best for us. Many people have our best interests in heart and are usually the source of indecision. I know these people don't intend to hurt us and I am convinced they have good intentions. Remember, look where we are and seek our influence's that got us here.

As to what others think of us... Who gives a crap? I'm not saying we should ignore, argue, disregard or stop loving them. Listen to them, but if they don't meet up with our inner beliefs then say something like "I have listened to what you say and will take that into thought". When they become persistent on recording their own beliefs onto you then say something like "I have listened to you many times and have yielded with negative results. I wish to continue our relationship and would appreciate it if we did not discuss this topic any further". This may be of discomfort and some "friends" and family may slowly slip away. Don't waste time chasing the birds, keep focused on the crop.

Everything around us has always been and always will be. This isn't some aged old philosophy, it's just a fact. Think about it... It took a thought to cut a tree, then to cut it again, stand it upright, and BOOM!!! Wheels were invented. It took thought to mix already existing elements together to make bricks for houses, iron for nails, coal to burn for fuel, blades to cut, wood for matches, and hair for rope. It took thought to use the elements of our earth to our advantage… fire to boil water, water to drink and also to sail on, wind to move giant ships, and the stars to guide sailors through the night. EVERYTHING, I mean EVERYTHING was once a thought. Using what always has been and what always will be is the 'secret' to self-ambition. So, I ask that you take a deep hard look at yourself and realize you control your own thoughts. Therefore, who gives a crap about what others think? Stop letting other people's thoughts influence your own. Stop allowing negativity to influence your thinking. You should now realize that a simple shift in thought can drastically change your life. Ask yourself, what do you think about? What influences your thinking? Where are your influences coming from? Should you and how are you going to change them? One thought will truly change your life; take ACTION ACTION ACTION!!!

TREE THEORY

I magine if you will, the might of a great oak tree. One that boasts a hundred years plus in age. Roots embedded deep into the ground. Sprouts as high as New York's skyline. Now visualize the roots. A woven web of complex strings that feed the mighty oak whilst keeping the oak stable as if the foundation of a great mansion. Roots dug deep in dirt, grasping, sucking water from the earth that surrounds its heavy bark. These roots represent the importance of knowledge, knowing where you have come from. For each one of us has a story. Some are good, others not. Nonetheless, we all have a story. Roots lay the foundation of life. They cannot be changed. For some this may be a harsh awakening. The truth is they will stay forever. Roots feed off the earth, supplying life with all vital nutrients. Here it is time to make a choice. Either allow the roots to feed you all the nasty gravel and muddy water, reminiscing and gripping onto horrible, ill-feeling memories of the past. OR, remembering the strength and knowledge earned from each unique life lesson. The key to moving forward is learning the importance of never forgetting the past.

The trunk, a mighty girth of the oak. The most visible yet punished asset of the tree. The trunk sees insects climbing up and down, feeding on the crevasses of each bark implant. A woodpecker that chooses to dis-body the bark, pecking away one head-bob at a time. Weathering of the rain, winds, and beams of the sun bouncing off the trunk. The trunk stands strong representing the present, where you are right now.

How much good or bad nutrition have you absorbed led you to where you are today? A weak trunk sees the tree fall. A strong trunk will absorb beaten after beaten and yet flourish like a well-presented mighty oak. Look back to seek guidance and deposit it into your future. Stay focused, look forward. Driving with a blindfold on is a certain way to crash. Take note of how a tree grows. There are NO limits to its height. We must do the same by making sure the tracks of our goals head only up. I recall once when I was a young boy, we were walking to a park to fly our kites. I was looking down at the ground, lost in my own thoughts, thinking to myself that my kite was going to fly higher than everyone else's. I walked right into a street lamp. After seeking medical attention and having the other kids laugh at me, I sat out and missed the opportunity to fly my kite. Lesson learned: I may have had (and I did) the best kite that day, yet with my head down, I never got the chance to fly it. Walking with your head down may find you pennies but walking with your head up will find you riches. How many times have you walked with your head down? How many kites have you not flown? How much potential is clinging to your life, yet you've continuously looked down? Think seriously about this. Take some time right now to think and write of these missed opportunities. Most people can relate when I say we've all looked back on our lives and realized we've missed opportunities. Part is because we didn't know what we have in front of us. The other part, people are afraid to take risks. Generate new thoughts, tighten the screw to secure your future. It takes many years for a tree to grow strong. Patience and nutrition are the keys to strength and healthy growth.

Branches and leaves represent where you are heading. Sometimes the wind will come and strip the healthiest of Oaks of its leaf's. Sometimes leaves just fall. Allow the wind to come and take the leaves. Trees grow new leaves. The branches remain strong. It is in the branches that we bear the fruit of our knowledge, time, past, lessons, and labor. Ironically leaves display visible satisfaction of hard work, which, if used right, will provide shade from scorching mid-summers sun which threatens to weaken the bark of might Oak.

CONFUSION VS
DISCIPLINE

A burning desire crawls through the veins whilst a fire of confusion itches the mind. This causes conflict in a man's true direction. As I sit here writing my thoughts and philosophy on paper, I glance at my liquor cabinet debating whether to have a drink or not. You see I am a creature of habit, and for a few years of my life I have allowed some bad habits to break me. One drink turns into two and three, and the next thing I know I'm 40lbs overweight trying to live in the past. I took some unique courses to change my relationship with all my bad habits. I even reached out for help by checking into a rehab center that I now label 'mental health boot camp'. It's okay to take a knee and ask for help. As I have previously stated, I'm trying to figure out this life just like any other. One of the course's instructors made a claim regarding alcohol which got me thinking. He said "you can choose to only have one drink, but that's the only choice you have". What he was alluding to is that after you make that choice, the habit takes over. Good or bad, it will take over. This got me thinking about the other choices we make. If our only choice is one drink, surely our only choice is to save a dollar, do one push up, take one walk, say one thank you. If our only choice is the first, then shouldn't we make the first count? My choice was to type one more word and bring these ideas to you. By changing my relationship with my bad habits, replacing them with well-structured disciplined habits, I choose to live the life I desire.

I tell you this not as an excuse for addiction. And if you are struggling with addiction, I urge you to seek professional help. I tell you this as it is my belief that we all have moments of confusion vs discipline and when those moments present themselves, it's time to act. Even if it hurts, itches the mind, drives you momentarily crazy, keep acting on disciplined choices. Acting as if, before you receive your blessings, it is hard. Look at actors. Some of them become a whole other person when assuming a role. They practice their acting over and over again until they become unrecognizable. The age-old adjective 'fake it till you make it' combined with 'practice makes perfect' works.

Learn to keep your head down and your eyes up. Look up. Remain focused and remember nothing good comes to those who are not willing to grind.

IT'S NEVER TOO LATE TO CHANGE

C hange is welcomed by those who are suffering. In a world where success is defined as the amount of fame, likes, re-tweets, and money we can quickly assemble as young as possible, many people feel they missed their train. History tells us another story. KFC founder Colonel Sanders was in his 60s when he made his millions. Samuel Jackson was in his 40's when he became a famous actor. These examples can be seen all over history. By the time someone approaches their forties, they feel it's too late and life is nearing the end. Let us disband this notion and break it down. From birth to our early twenties should be the time we learn. We go to school, we observe others, listen to ideas and take it all in. Now some of us including myself play catch up and go to college later in life; that's okay. However, the best time to learn is while the system sends you to school. Early twenties to early thirty's are where most people make their mistakes. They get in debt, marry and divorce, and make mistakes. As we have learned, mistakes are okay. Now some people do great here, others not so well. Now remember that as we approach our forties, we should take 39 years of lessons and go for it. Most millionaires make their money in their forties.

That's how it's supposed to be. I call this the concession of life. There was an article once in The Daily Mail titled "They say life ends at forty, now forty is where it begins". Stop thinking you've missed the train. There is no train, only opportunity. Sunlight is gold to the man living in the dark.

THE TRUE COST

We've heard it all before: nothing in life is free. The cost of self-worth, ambition, and success is priceless. Changing who you are today to what you want to be tomorrow is priceless. The startup cost is heavy, and I don't mean in dollars. The mental and physical process you will surely go through is overwhelmingly heavy. Persistence will ease the pain as you become stronger and more knowledgeable. It truly is like riding a bike. Remember how sore your backside was after being in that seat? Remember the bruised feeling in between your legs? After a while it slowly faded away as your body adjusted. The cost of development is equal. Your ego will be bruised, your body sore, and your mind muddled. All that will settle as your mind, body, and soul get used to your new way of life. There will be late nights and early mornings as you scramble for time to complete your newfound habits. Tackle the morning well and you've set yourself up for the day. No successful person wakes up after 6 am. Let that sink in. Associates and friends will disappear as the new you step out in front of life. You will be misunderstood by many. What you are doing will look and sound weird to others. Many people will try and drag you back. You will now find yourself attached to the bungee cord of life. A few bounces will happen. You must fight the cord so that you never find your way back to where you just came from. The only way back is for someone to pull you up and trust me, they will try. Many people on this path find themselves lonely, unless they find someone who understands real ambition. People want you to do good but never better than them. And it simply comes down to their lack of knowledge and understanding. For these reasons and many more, you will do many things alone. Loneliness is more peaceful than regret. The explorer finds himself lonely not for long.

I hope and have faith that this book opens your eyes to an understanding of how this all works. It doesn't always work like this and will often fail. That's part of it. I'm by far an expert on life, and I'm just trying to be the best I can be all the time. I do understand that we are all presented with the same elements. Some will use the elements, some will throw them away, others will curse them out, and most will just plod along unaware of their existence. I ask you to take what you have and use it. I believe the human race is a unique one. We can stare at all other species all day long, and it's the human race that has been given the gift of thought. The Bible says man was created by God in his image. Let me leave you with this… A few years back, when I was eighteen years old, I was dating a girl. I decided one Christmas to ask her to marry me. While still in school, my sister worked in a jewelry shop to save some money. I got with my sister and brought a gorgeous engagement ring for her. We still had a few months left until Christmas and I needed a place to hide the ring, so I settled for her underwear drawer. Why? Because I was very aware that if you are not looking for some-thing, then you will not find it. True to my belief, she never found the ring. How many rings in your life are you not finding? How many rings are right in front of you and you just don't see them? Talents, ideas, creations, betterments, they are all in front of you. You just have to look. Let the words of this book spill out onto the dry desserts of ill thoughts and actions and allow faith to prevail. It was once said that God had to find a place to hide man's greatest treasure. Where better to hide it than in man's own mind?

Made in the USA
Columbia, SC
29 April 2024

35042847R00090